Interview
with
the Devil

Interview
with
the Devil

What Satan would say
(if he ever told the truth)

Russell Wight

BARBOUR
PUBLISHING

Print ISBN 978-1-61626-662-2

eBook Editions:
Adobe Digital Edition (.epub) 978-1-60742-057-6
Kindle and MobiPocket Edition (.prc) 978-1-60742-045-3

Published by Barbour Publishing, Inc., P.O. Box 719,
Uhrichsville, Ohio 44683, www.barbourbooks.com

*Our mission is to publish and distribute inspirational products
offering exceptional value and biblical encouragement to the masses.*

Member of the
Evangelical Christian
Publishers Association

Printed in the United States of America.

CONTENTS

1.

INTRODUCTION

The evil one is known by many names—first as Lucifer, then Satan. He has been given titles such as the prince of demons and prince of the power of the air. He has been given descriptive names, such as the great serpent and the dragon, and names reflective of his character, such as the accuser. He is most often called the devil. For this reporter, the name that stands out the most is the one used by Jesus and found in the Gospel of John. Jesus was responding to some Jewish leaders, known as the Pharisees, who had accused Him of being demon-possessed.

> Jesus said to them, "If God were your
> Father, you would love me, for I have
> come here from God. I have not come on
> my own; God sent me. Why is my lan-
> guage not clear to you? Because you are
> unable to hear what I say. You belong to
> your father, the devil, and you want to
> carry out your father's desires. He was a
> murderer from the beginning, not hold-
> ing to the truth, for there is no truth in
> him. When he lies, he speaks his native
> language, for he is a liar and the father
> of lies. Yet because I tell the truth, you do
> not believe me! Can any of you prove me
> guilty of sin? If I am telling the truth,
> why don't you believe me? Whoever be-
> longs to God hears what God says. The
> reason you do not hear is that you do not
> belong to God."
>
> JOHN 8:42–47

As Jesus spoke with the Pharisees, He
recognized something in their speech—
the same patterns and manipulations that
He'd heard from another adversary: Satan. It was in this moment that He named

these Pharisees children of the devil. He then described the evil one in terms that are clear and concise: The devil is a liar and the father of lies. When anyone considers the idea of Satan, they must begin with this foundational truth from Jesus Christ.

But imagine now, if for a short time, the devil—Satan—the father of lies, were capable of speaking *only the truth*. It's an impossibility, of course. But it's an interesting and helpful way to see through the untruths the devil speaks to confuse people and ruin lives. That's the whole idea of this book—that Satan *must* say what's really in his heart. For example,

Human, I hate you. I despise you, just as I despise the God who created you in His image and formed you in your mother's womb. I want your life on earth to be miserable and your eternity to be spent in the lake of fire. I want to fill your days and nights with temptation and sin so you can mock and oppose God, just like me. I want you to give in to the desires of your flesh—to serve me rather than Him. You see, by doing so, you will grieve and hurt God.

I really am the roaring lion, and I wish nothing more than to devour you, to shoot fiery darts at you, to convince you that the Word of God cannot be trusted. I want you to believe that God is not love, that Christ is not your advocate, and that the Holy Spirit cannot keep you safely in His care. I want you to doubt everything God has said and everything He has done.

I am a schemer, always working and planning to own every human as my disciple. You see, "I will ascend to the heavens; I will raise my throne above the stars of God; I will sit enthroned on the mount of assembly, on the utmost heights of Mount Zaphon. I will ascend above the tops of the clouds; I will make myself like the Most High."[1]

In the format of a long interview between a news reporter and the devil, this book will take you through the major Bible passages where the enemy of God, the created angel known as Satan, appears. You will hear his honest explanations of these historical events. In a later chapter, you will hear the devil's commentary on four New Testament writers who have given specific information on how to resist his schemes.

Realize that Satan was not always God's enemy. He began as Lucifer, likely the most gifted of the created angels. At some point, sin was found in him and he conspired with other angels against God. In the New Testament, He is often called the *devil*, a Greek word which means "accuser" or "maligner." In the Old Testament, he was known as *Satan*, a Hebrew word which means "adversary" or "opponent."

- He opposed God by taking the form of a serpent and deceiving Adam and Eve.

- He opposed God by challenging the motives and lifestyle of a man named Job.

- He opposed God by leveling accusations against a Jewish high priest named Joshua.

- He opposed God by tempting Jesus Christ in the wilderness.

- He opposed God by tempting followers of Christ to commit sinful deeds.

- He opposes God today by attacking believers in Jesus Christ, and by also clouding the truth about Jesus Christ with those who do not yet know Christ as Savior.

- He will oppose God on earth in the future by twice leading open rebellions among humans—once before the Second Coming of Jesus Christ and once following the completion of Christ's thousand-year reign on earth.

One day, the devil's opposition to God will lead to punishment, a fire which will torment him throughout eternity.

Though the interviews you are about to read are fictional, the story of Satan—his history, his current activities, and his future punishment—is clearly told in God's Word, the Bible. Test what you read in this book against what you see in the scriptures—and be prepared to battle the enemy of your soul.

Scripture references

[1]Isaiah 14:13–14

2.

HEADLINE:
REBELLION

At some point in history before the creation of Adam and Eve, God, in His wisdom, created a group of spirit beings. At their creation, all of them—angels, cherubim, and seraphim—were dedicated servants of the Most High; however, one of these beings, originally known as Lucifer, was filled with pride and found to be evil. He led a rebellion against God, taking with him many spirit beings we now refer to as "demons." This rebellion is described in the Old Testament prophecies of Isaiah and Ezekiel, as follows:

The word of the LORD came to me: "Son of man, take up a lament concerning the king of Tyre and say to him: 'This is what the Sovereign LORD says:

"You were the seal of perfection, full of wisdom and perfect in beauty.

"You were in Eden, the garden of God; every precious stone adorned you: carnelian, chrysolite and emerald, topaz, onyx and jasper, lapis lazuli, turquoise and beryl. Your settings and mountings were made of gold; on the day you were created they were prepared.

"You were anointed as a guardian cherub, for so I ordained you. You were on the holy mount of God; you walked among the fiery stones.

"You were blameless in your ways from the day you were created till wickedness was found in you.

"Through your widespread trade you were filled with violence, and you sinned. So I drove you in disgrace from the mount of God, and I expelled you, guardian cherub, from among the fiery stones.

"Your heart became proud on account of your beauty, and you corrupted your wisdom because of your splendor. So I threw you to the earth; I made a spectacle of you before kings.

"By your many sins and dishonest trade
you have desecrated your sanctuaries. So I
made a fire come out from you, and it con-
sumed you, and I reduced you to ashes on the
ground in the sight of all who were watching.

"All the nations who knew you are ap-
palled at you; you have come to a horrible
end and will be no more.' "

EZEKIEL 28:11–19

How you have fallen from heaven, morning
star, son of the dawn! You have been cast down
to the earth, you who once laid low the nations!

You said in your heart, "I will ascend
to the heavens; I will raise my throne above
the stars of God; I will sit enthroned on the
mount of assembly, on the utmost heights of
Mount Zaphon.

I will ascend above the tops of the clouds; I
will make myself like the Most High."

But you are brought down to the realm of
the dead, to the depths of the pit.

Those who see you stare at you, they
ponder your fate: "Is this the man who shook
the earth and made kingdoms tremble, the
man who made the world a wilderness, who
overthrew its cities and would not let his
captives go home?"

ISAIAH 14:12 –17

This reporter was curious about the devil's rebellion against God. So I asked for an explanation of the devil's life before his rebellion and for his thoughts while the rebellion was taking place.

Yes, I did indeed lead a rebellion against God.

You see, I had an important role among all of the spirit-beings. I was the guardian. I, the most adorned, was decked out in precious stones mounted in gold. Not only was I the most beautiful of all the created beings, I worked in the most beautiful of all places—on the height of God's mountain, among the fiery stones, in the very presence of God. I was the protector of the throne of God—no other spirit-being would have access to God without being in my presence as well. I did everything that God had required of me and worshipped Him with every part of my being. I did it all with precision and perfection.

Then one day I realized how much

greater I was than all the other spirit-beings. I realized that the amount of wisdom, majesty, and beauty I had, as well as the work I had accomplished, was greater than all others. In that moment I thought to myself, I should be in charge of everything. I should be the Most High. Still, the focus of every eye, every conversation, and every moment of worship was on God. Suddenly everything became quite clear to me. I just could not allow it to continue. The focus needed to shift from God to me.

From that moment on I began plotting my rebellion. It was easy to convince so many of the weak-minded beings to follow me as I launched a revolution against God. They would follow any pretty face—so it might as well be mine. I declared myself as worthy of being God. With all my wisdom and beauty, I could do and be everything. My objective was simple: to turn the worship and focus of all assembled beings from God to me. They would seek my wisdom and follow my commands, not God's.

At this point, I ceased to live for God and began to live for me. In all my perfection, beauty, splendor, and pride I realized in my heart of hearts that God did not know what was best for me, or anyone else. But I did. I would have control over destiny. I would have control over all.

Of course, you know that I was defeated in this initial assault. What I hoped would be a quick victory against God has become a long war of attrition. I win some battles and I lose some battles. Many of these are detailed in God's book, and doubtless I will be asked about them in this interview. You should understand that the battles—some over the souls of humans, others among powers in the heavenly realms—never end. I often find myself personally squared against Michael, the archangel who once served under my command and now stands as God's most competent servant. If you have read God's book, you know that

Michael and I had a very intense battle over the dead body of Moses.[1] But that's another story.

Since my rebellion, I have spent the years attempting to thwart God's plans at every turn. I have legions of spirit-beings, or angels, who follow me—God's scriptures call them demons, rulers, powers of this dark world, and spiritual forces of evil. We have been banished, forced out of our rightful place among the fiery stones and left to do whatever we can to bring misery to God.

Although I lost my original fight and realize I may never rule every created being, my hatred for God and my desire to cause Him grief remains. Therefore, I will fight any fight so that I may defeat God in every battle. I may not rule the universe—but I will attempt to rule every piece of creation I can. Including you.

Scripture references
[1]Jude 9

3.
HEADLINE:
DECEPTION

The first humans to walk the earth were placed by God in a perfect place and in a perfect state. Best of all, they were in a perfect relationship with God. The adversary, the one who had been cast out of heaven, took the form of a serpent ("that ancient serpent called the devil, or Satan" in Revelation 12:9) and set out to destroy the perfect place and state God had created. The Bible's opening chapters, more specifically Genesis 2 and 3, contain the record of these events.

The Lord God took the man and put him in the Garden of Eden to work it and take care of it. And the Lord God commanded the man, "You are free to eat from any tree in the garden; but you must not eat from the tree of the knowledge of good and evil, for when you eat from it you will certainly die."

GENESIS 2:15–17

Now the serpent was more crafty than any of the wild animals the Lord God had made. He said to the woman, "Did God really say, 'You must not eat from any tree in the garden'?"

The woman said to the serpent, "We may eat fruit from the trees in the garden, but God did say, 'You must not eat fruit from the tree that is in the middle of the garden, and you must not touch it, or you will die.'"

"You will not certainly die," the serpent said to the woman. "For God knows that when you eat from it your eyes will be opened, and you will be like God, knowing good and evil."

When the woman saw that the fruit of the tree was good for food and pleasing to the eye, and also desirable for gaining wisdom, she took some and ate it. She also gave some to her husband, who was with her, and he ate it. Then the eyes of both of them were

opened, and they realized they were naked;
so they sewed fig leaves together and made
coverings for themselves.

Then the man and his wife heard the
sound of the LORD God as he was walking
in the garden in the cool of the day, and they
hid from the LORD God among the trees of
the garden. But the LORD God called to the
man, "Where are you?"

He answered, "I heard you in the garden,
and I was afraid because I was naked; so I hid."

And he said, "Who told you that you
were naked? Have you eaten from the tree
that I commanded you not to eat from?"

The man said, "The woman you put here
with me—she gave me some fruit from the
tree, and I ate it."

Then the LORD God said to the woman,
"What is this you have done?"

The woman said, "The serpent deceived
me, and I ate."

GENESIS 3:1–13

This reporter brought these passages
from Genesis to the "ancient serpent" and
asked for his impressions as God spoke the
world into existence and of the devil's interaction with the man and the woman in
the Garden of Eden.

All of the spirit-beings, whether the cherubim and seraphim and other angels still following God or the demons following me, watched intently as God spent what you know as six days speaking the physical world into existence. The cherubim and angels just kept worshipping and praising God with each word He uttered, with each part of the universe that appeared out of nothing. My followers and I found the display impressive to be sure, but completely unnecessary. What is the point of all these physical items when our spiritual world and its beings, like me, are so wondrous?

Every twenty-four hours, God produced new stuff and then pronounced what he had made as "good." Yet I did not see anything that compared to my beauty. A sun and a moon—they were nothing compared to me. Flowers! Trees! Land and seas! Pathetic! All of God's words seemed like foolish prattle, creating nothing of consequence.

But things got a little more

interesting on day five. The birds and fish seemed to have possibilities. Maybe with a little work they could become something to be used against God in my rebellion. Perhaps they would choose to worship me and follow my plans. Perhaps they could be manipulated to disobey God's law, to dismiss the greatness of their Creator.

As I explored these creatures, I found that they operated only on instinct and by rote, really nothing I could use in another assault on the throne of God. They had no potential, no personal understanding, no capacity to be anything more than what God had created them to be. They didn't even seem to be aware of their own existence. Unlike the spirit-beings, the creatures had no greatness within them.

Everything changed on that sixth day, though. The various wild animals were of little interest, but the two-legged ones were different. They had a quality about them that was hard to miss, much more than the beasts on the

27

land, the birds of the air, or the fish in the seas. For example, the beasts typically only made a single noise when they were startled or when they wanted something. The birds would sing to each other, but it was the same song over and over. The fish seemed to move about in totally random patterns. However, the two-legged beings seemed to move about with purpose. They used many different words and seemed to have a range of emotions. They laughed. They sang. Their conversation showed intellect and a capacity to grow and develop and learn. These two-legged beings, while not as majestic, seemed to have many of the qualities as the spirit-beings among which I lived.

Upon closer inspection, I was sickened by what I found—these things were made in God's image. These beings were created with personality, individuality, and given the ability to think and to make choices. My legions of demons and I came to realize that the two-legged ones were created to be like

God, with their three distinct parts—
a body to house them, a spirit to drive
them, and a soul to connect them to
God. Of all that God had made, these
humans were unique, actually created
to be better than spirit-beings. It
all had to do with that soul of theirs.

I decided right then and there that
I would not rest until I found a way to
destroy these things—the man and the
woman. I especially wanted to destroy
their souls. No created being anywhere
was going to have the capacity to be
greater than me.

The man and the woman were eager to
obey God and please Him, just as I had
been. They worshipped His name. They
sang songs about Him, songs which they
wrote themselves. They took pleasure
in caring for the plants and the animals God had created. They even took
daily walks with God each evening after their work was finished. God had
declared the two-legged beings to be
"very good," and it was obvious that He
loved them. When God walked with them,

He would appear in the form of a man and tell them of His great love for them. The two-leggeds would, in turn, express their own love for God, bowing on their knees before Him and thanking Him for His good and perfect gifts. Most evenings, I could not bear to watch them together. I simply wanted to destroy this love fest, to ruin this existence for both God and the two-leggeds.

So I began scheming. How could I make these humans disappoint God and cause Him to no longer love them? I devised a plan, taking several weeks before finally deciding I would need to get one of them alone at some point in the early afternoon, a time when they would be hungry. It did not matter which one I picked; I knew I'd only need one attempt.

Now, which of the rules God had given them would they be most likely to disobey? Since there were only a handful of rules, I would have to choose carefully.

The two-leggeds were to multiply. I certainly did not want there to be more of these disgusting beings, especially since the purpose of their existence was to worship God. I suppose I could keep them from multiplying, but as the animals and the birds and the fish were already having offspring, I knew the humans would not be far behind.

They were to rule over the animals. That could be used to my advantage. Perhaps they could be abusive to their charges or misuse them in some way. Perhaps the humans could be made to be angry at an animal then kill it. That could evoke the wrath of God. Or maybe I could get one of the two-leggeds to be critical of God because of an animal's supposed imperfection.

The humans were also to eat from the plants God had made. But I seem to recall Him designating one tree in the middle of the garden as off-limits. He called it the "tree of the knowledge of good and evil."[1] Observing the man and the woman, I finally determined that this was where I could trap them. I could convince them that God was keeping them in the dark, not allowing them to know everything they needed to know. Perhaps I could convince the man that God was holding him back, not giving him the full authority that he needed to have true dominion over the earth. Perhaps I could convince the woman that she needed more from life. After all, she was only a "helper" to the man. Maybe there was pride in these beings, just like there was in me.

I decided then and there I would tempt them with the notion that they could—and should—be like God, knowing everything He knows. I would pander to their pride.

I just had to wait for the right moment. And then it came.

One afternoon, the woman, whom the man had named Eve, sat down to rest near the tree that was off-limits. The man himself, named Adam, was nearby tending to some shrub, but clearly paying attention to the woman.

Observing her, I could tell that she was hungry, so I entered the body of a nearby serpent and moved over to talk to her. I had previously observed that she had great fascination with the serpent, that she had found it to be beautiful with its ability to move so gracefully among the trees and the plants due to its strong legs and to consume vegetables with its powerful jaws. It was a crafty creature. And although other animals did not instinctually know when the serpent was present, Eve knew. I did not believe she would be alarmed if one of these creatures would suddenly open its mouth and begin to speak.

I had determined to confuse these two-leggeds about what God had really said and what God had really meant in His rules. Upon arriving, I asked a simple question to see if Eve truly understood the rule God had given. As I surmised, she was not at all surprised by a talking serpent—she answered right away that she understood God's edict. As she continued to speak, I discovered that she and Adam had added their own extra rule. You see, God never told them they could not touch the tree in the middle of the garden, only that they could not eat the fruit. Very wise of them to decide to not even touch the tree, but when the woman misspoke, adding her own little caveat, I knew I would be able to convince her to break God's rule.

So I appealed to her pride: Did she really think God would kill her? Wasn't God holding out on her? Didn't she want to know as much as God knew? I got her thinking about what she did not have. She looked at the fruit, and it did look good to her. She thought about the potential for understanding then she reached out, took some of the fruit, and held it up to her face. She breathed deeply then took a bite. She ate it all. Then she took another piece of fruit to the man, who had been listening all along, and he gladly ate, too. The deed was done—and it was the most satisfaction I had ever felt. I had tricked the beings God had created! They had disobeyed God, and that would cause Him great pain.

When God came looking for the humans that evening, He found them hiding in fear, knowing they had violated His rule. I took great satisfaction watching God curse the ground. It warmed my heart to see the majestic serpent being made to crawl on the ground and become one the most despised of all the animals as deadly venom filled his powerful jaws. I felt a surge of victory as I witnessed God driving the man and the woman out of the garden.

Some time later, I took great pleasure watching the man have to deal with the thorns and the weeds as he attempted to harvest food. I tingled with delight in hearing the woman scream in pain as she gave birth to a baby boy. Her shrieks were music to my ears!

I laughed as God grieved over the sin committed by the offspring of the man and the woman, until finally He had to destroy their descendents in a flood, leaving one family and a few animals on a large boat. I had wreaked havoc on God's creation, and I would lie in wait until another opportunity presented itself.

Scripture references
[1]Genesis 2:17

4.
HEADLINE:
ATTACK

The scriptures introduce us to a man named Job. He was a wealthy man with a loving wife and many children. Job was also a dedicated worshipper of God. The adversary, Satan, came before God and offered a theory: Job only worshipped and served God because of God's hand of protection over Job. God decided to prove to His adversary that that theory was wrong. So, at first, God allowed Satan to attack Job's family and possessions only:

*One day the angels came to present them-
selves before the LORD, and Satan also came
with them. The LORD said to Satan, "Where
have you come from?"*

*Satan answered the LORD, "From
roaming throughout the earth, going back
and forth on it."*

*Then the LORD said to Satan, "Have you
considered my servant Job? There is no one
on earth like him; he is blameless and upright, a man who fears God and shuns evil."*

*"Does Job fear God for nothing?" Satan
replied. "Have you not put a hedge around
him and his household and everything he has?
You have blessed the work of his hands, so that
his flocks and herds are spread throughout
the land. But now stretch out your hand and
strike everything he has, and he will surely
curse you to your face."*

*The LORD said to Satan, "Very well,
then, everything he has is in your power, but
on the man himself do not lay a finger."*

*Then Satan went out from the presence
of the LORD.*

JOB 1:6–12

After he learned that all his children were
dead and all his possessions destroyed, Job
praised the name of the Lord. So Satan

returned to God's presence with another accusation: that Job only worshipped God because he still had his health. God permitted Satan to attack Job again.

On another day the angels came to present themselves before the LORD, and Satan also came with them to present himself before him. And the LORD said to Satan, "Where have you come from?"

Satan answered the LORD, "From roaming throughout the earth, going back and forth on it."

Then the LORD said to Satan, "Have you considered my servant Job? There is no one on earth like him; he is blameless and upright, a man who fears God and shuns evil. And he still maintains his integrity, though you incited me against him to ruin him without any reason."

"Skin for skin!" Satan replied. "A man will give all he has for his own life. But now stretch out your hand and strike his flesh and bones, and he will surely curse you to your face."

The LORD said to Satan, "Very well, then, he is in your hands; but you must spare his life."

So Satan went out from the presence of the LORD and afflicted Job with painful sores from the soles of his feet to the crown of his head. Then Job took a piece of broken pottery and scraped himself with it as he sat among the ashes.

His wife said to him, "Are you still maintaining your integrity? Curse God and die!"

He replied, "You are talking like a foolish woman. Shall we accept good from God, and not trouble?"

In all this, Job did not sin in what he said.

JOB 2:1–10

This reporter asked Satan to explain some of the unanswered questions from this ancient story: Why does Satan still appear before God? What was so fascinating about Job? Despite Satan's best efforts, Job remained faithful to God. How did this defeat affect Satan in his battle against God?

I am a keen observer of events that are happening on the earth. Through my network of spirit-beings stationed throughout the globe, I am alerted to anything of interest—anything unusual or of note. For the most part, these two-legged creatures pursue their own interests and ignore their Creator. This delights me for it grieves God. Even though most of the world's population worships something other than the God of heaven (and thus is really worshipping me), on occasion there will be men and women—and at times entire communities—who will worship God with all their heart and all their soul and all their mind. Yet there are times when even the best of these believers relax, let down their guard. With my network of spies, we miss nothing. Our ongoing battle with God demands that we be vigilant, ready to attack any person at any moment, especially those who make the worship of God a priority.

On occasion, and only when necessary, I return to my former residence among the fiery stones, what you think of as "heaven." (May I mention again my belief that only I in my beauty am fit among all the created beings to walk among the fiery stones?) The angels who remained loyal to God during the rebellion are constantly coming before Him, worshipping and singing and bowing. All of it makes me sick. I want them to worship me. Painful as it is for me to return there with God in control, it is logical for me to visit, to see what I can learn, to see if there are any new plans or ideas being brought from the mind of God.

As much as it pains me, when God summons me to His throne room, something inside me compels me to go. Though I no longer serve His desires or His wishes, I still have to show up when called and give a report of my activities. I tell Him exactly what I think of these pitiful humans He has created and how they only serve Him because of His goodness to them. I tell God that it is my goal to destroy every last one of those who choose to worship Him, and how I and my demons work every day to blind those who might someday choose to worship Him. Yes, we do speak about specific humans—and on one particular day, He mentioned the name of Job.

We had been observing the human named Job for decades. It was no surprise to me when God mentioned him. God always points out His followers to me, just as I point out the ones who follow after me, the number of whom increases daily. My path is broad—why, a human can choose just about any lifestyle and be a follower of mine. God's path is so narrow. Confessing sin and begging for forgiveness, in my enlightened opinion, is no way to live.

For example, consider the days of rain. God was so angry with the people He created that He decided to destroy them and start over. He only saved Noah and seven members of Noah's family. Put them on a big boat and then flooded everything else. Think of how effective I am—Noah preached about God's judgment for 120 years and, except for his family, he had zero converts. Zip, nada, and zilch. What a great victory for me that no one listened to Noah! Every human, except the eight on the boat, followed my broad path.

Think, too, about the nation of Israel. Abraham, the first patriarch of Israel, failed to trust God on several occasions. He and his wife, Sarah, just could not wait for God to provide them with a baby—so Abraham, prompted by Sarah (and yours truly), went out and made one with an Egyptian slave. Priceless! Jacob, Abraham's grandson, was a deceiver—just like me. He stole all that rightfully belonged to his brother, and did it with the help of his mommy! Then he went and cheated his father-in-law, who in turn cheated Jacob. These are my kind of two-legged beings!

Jacob's children then tramped off to Egypt, following Joseph. There the Israelites eventually found themselves slaves to the pharaohs—and it took them several hundred years before they finally cried out to God. Isn't that pathetic? After their cry for deliverance, God brought them out of Egypt by killing thousands more of His humans.

Then what did His "special" people

do? Made an idol—a golden cow—and worshipped it. I've been in God's presence—trust me, He looks and acts nothing like a cow! These humans can be manipulated so easily. Constantly choosing the broad path, the easy way, rather than confessing their sins to God. All the better for me. I gladly accept their worship in whatever form they choose to give it.

So this Job person worships God every day. He offers sacrifices as payment for his own sins—and the sins of his children. But why wouldn't he? God blessed everything Job put his hand to. His family was healthy and wealthy—not as much as a single injury or illness and never a day when they were hungry or thirsty. His crops always succeeded. His animals always produced. From my perspective, it's no wonder he worshipped God every day. Job lived the perfect life—for a human.

The first time God asked me about Job, I was ready with an answer. "Of course Job serves God. . .his life is

45

perfect. Take away his stuff, leave him poor and broken, and Job will be like most other men. He will cease his worship."

So God took away His hedge of protection and gave me access to everything Job loved. God often shows love to His followers by protecting them from my schemes and attacks, but this was not the first time God had allowed me to destroy one of His people. He says that at times His followers need to endure the testing of their faith. That's fine with me. I will gladly go on the attack since anything that hurts a follower of God ultimately hurts God—and that is my main motivation. So in one afternoon, I proceeded to destroy Job's family, his farm, his livestock, and his wealth. I took everything then waited for Job to curse God—and thereby worship me.

But I was stunned and horrified when that day ended. Job still worshipped God. He still offered sacrifices. Worst of all, he never sinned.

His children were all dead. He did not sin. His livestock was destroyed, his crops devastated. He did not sin. Day after day after day, Job continued to worship—and he did not sin. I wiped out everything Job loved, and he did not sin. How annoying.

Not long after my destruction of Job's family and wealth, I found myself summoned to the presence of God again. I knew God was going to ask about Job, because Job had remained true in his devotion to God and had not worshipped me. But I was ready with an answer.

This time, I told God that Job still served Him because he had his health. Men can live without children or possessions—because if they're healthy, they can always get more. Take away his health—make a man's entire existence about pain and suffering—and then watch him break. That was my challenge to God. Let me have Job's body and I know he'll abandon the worship of God. God agreed, but only up to a point. He

47

allowed me to attack Job's body, but not take his life.

No problem. I had seen many men and women ravaged with disease, much of which I caused personally. Disease is part of the curse God put on them after Eden. So I found the worst possible plague and brought that germ to Job. Not one inch of his body was spared! Job suffered an agony that gave me such satisfaction. Then I waited for the inevitable, confident Job would begin cursing God in the midst of his agony.

I cannot fully explain to you the crushing blow to my pride when Job did not stop worshipping God. I was so distraught, I did not even think to send Job's wife into the fray—you know, when she told him to "curse God and die."[1] She did that all on her own initiative. A girl after my own heart—like all you humans are, apart from God. But, still, Job never wavered in his faith. He continued to worship.

In this matter, I had failed. Job still worshipped God. Over the coming years, God returned Job's wealth and his health and gave him more children. It all just made me angry. I had lost a battle. The human stayed true. For me, Job is the one that got away.

But I keep reminding myself of the many who have betrayed God when they lost their health or their wealth or their family. So I will keep working to defeat God by destroying those that He loves.

Scripture references
[1] Job 2:9

5.
HEADLINE:
ACCUSATIONS

In the year 520 BC, the prophet Zechariah joined with a prophet named Haggai to encourage the people of Israel to repent of their sin and return to worshipping the God of Israel. Haggai preached four sermons. Zechariah was given a series of visions which illustrated God's plan for Israel at that time in history and in the future. One of those visions included a judge, a defendant, an advocate, and an accuser. The judge is the God of heaven. The defendant is Joshua, the name of the high priest in

Israel in 520 BC. The advocate is the angel of the Lord. The accuser is Satan.

This reporter recognizes that Satan is much more prominent in the books of the New Testament than the Old Testament. I asked God's adversary to give us information about the few times he does appear to challenge God's chosen nation—the descendents of Abraham, Isaac, and Jacob.

My name is not found as often in the "Old Testament" as it is in the "New." Other than what you have read so far, I am only mentioned in two other Old Testament verses. In both of those instances, I am standing up to God as His adversary, just as my name Satan implies.

Satan rose up against Israel and incited David to take a census of Israel.
                    1 CHRONICLES 21:1

Now there is a perfect example of my work among God's "chosen people": God wanted David to rely on Him—and I wanted David to rely on anything other than God. I convinced David to betray and disobey God. David followed my advice then had to confess his sin to God. Perfect.

Many Bible readers think that David's greatest sin was his adultery with Bathsheba—you know, that tryst that resulted in a pregnancy. To cover it up, David eventually arranged a situation where the woman's husband, Uriah, would be killed in battle. When the baby was born, it quickly died. . . and David wrote a song for Israel, expressing his remorse for violating God's law. Honestly, I had nothing to do with David's sin of adultery and murder—only two people died. Way too small for me.

If you read farther in 1 Chronicles 21, you'll find that as a result of David's sin of calling a census, the punishment from God was the death of seventy thousand men!

Appoint someone evil to oppose my enemy; let an accuser stand at his right hand.

PSALM 109:6

I guess David really had his fill of me when he wrote that song found in Psalm 109. He really understood what I wanted to accomplish. I am the "evil man" in that verse, the one who opposes anything God wants to do and anyone who wants to serve God. I am the one who seeks to disrupt and destroy that which God chooses to do in the life of His servant. And I did it to David—repeatedly.

In the only other place where I am explicitly mentioned in the Old Testament, I proudly played my role as accuser in the trial of a Jewish high priest named Joshua.

I must take a moment here to mention how much I hate the name Joshua. Of course, that is the name given to the Son of God at His birth as a human.

If you didn't know, the Hebrew name Yeshua gets translated into your English as Joshua. When the name Yeshua is translated into Greek, the language of the New Testament, it is *Ieesous* which is translated to Jesus in English. Ooh, it just makes me shudder.

So Joshua is a name I despise. That it is the Hebrew name of the Son of God during His time on earth makes it appalling to me. It was also the name of the son of Nun, the man who replaced Moses as leader of Israel when the nation occupied the land God gave to Abraham.

Okay. Enough of that. Back to the point at hand—my résumé! I'm very proud of my record of inciting people to sin. I was able to convince Cain to sin and murder his brother Abel. I was able to persuade the masses to sin then watched God destroy them all with a flood. I was able to induce Noah to sin after he left that boat, getting drunk and exposing his naked body to his family. What a picture of the preacher who spent 120 years building a floating zoo! So much for that "righteous man."[1]

In fact, I encouraged Abraham, Isaac, Jacob, Aaron (and most of the high priests), Moses, David (and most of the kings of Israel)—really, almost every person named by God in His book—to sin against God. Joshua the son of Nun, though. . .he could not be convinced. He stayed true and loyal to God throughout his life as a warrior and a politician. Did I mention that I hate the name Joshua?

But there's another prominent Joshua in God's book—the high priest from the time of the restoration of Israel. He worked with Governor Zerubbabel and the prophets Zechariah and Haggai as Israel returned to Jerusalem after the seventy years of captivity under Babylon and Persia. Those were seventy wonderful years for me, as no one was sacrificing to God in Jerusalem or worshipping Him in Galilee.

There were a few godly people, like Daniel and Mordecai, who I tried to have killed, but otherwise, it was a quiet seventy years. When the Jewish people were allowed to return, I encouraged their selfishness. They built their own houses, businesses, and lives, but they did not build a temple where they could meet together and worship God. The prophets blamed this sin on Zerubbabel and Joshua. When I was given the opportunity to accuse Joshua of his sins before God, I was pleased to do so. After all, Joshua was guilty—and I love accusing God's people.

So here's the passage, the only other place where I am clearly mentioned in the Old Testament. Oh, and just as a reminder, the players in this scene are: the judge as God; the defendant, Joshua; the advocate, the angel of the Lord; and me in my recurring role as the accuser.

Then [an instructing angel] showed me Joshua the high priest standing before the angel of the LORD, and Satan standing at his right side to accuse him. The LORD said to Satan, "The LORD rebuke you, Satan! The LORD, who has chosen Jerusalem, rebuke you! Is not this man a burning stick snatched from the fire?"

> *Now Joshua was dressed in filthy clothes as he stood before the angel. The angel said to those who were standing before him, "Take off his filthy clothes."*
>
> *Then he said to Joshua, "See, I have taken away your sin, and I will put fine garments on you."*
>
> *Then I [Zechariah] said, "Put a clean turban on his head." So they put a clean turban on his head and clothed him, while the angel of the LORD stood by.*
>
> *The angel of the LORD gave this charge to Joshua: "This is what the LORD Almighty says: 'If you will walk in obedience to me and keep my requirements, then you will govern my house and have charge of my courts, and I will give you a place among these standing here.'"*
>
> ZECHARIAH 3:1–7

Here's the lowdown from my point of view. In this scene, a court of law was set up and the prophet Zechariah was permitted to watch. Joshua the high priest stood in the middle of the room. I had dressed him in filthy garments—think of the worst smell, taste, and mess you've ever known, and you'll get close to what I put on that sinner. I wanted God to see exactly the kind of man who was serving as high priest. This Joshua was ready to be sentenced, just like I had been, for His crimes against God.

Just as God had rebuked Adam in the garden, I expected the Lord to rebuke Joshua. But God instead chose to rebuke me. He decided not to punish the high priest for his sins. I had watched God punish sinner after sinner over those four thousand years, but now He was choosing mercy and forgiveness! It was disgusting.

I brooded in silence as the filthy clothes I had so brazenly placed on Joshua were removed. The advocate, appearing here to be an angel, placed perfectly clean clothes on Joshua. I showed God a high priest stained with sin, and God showed me a high priest whose sins had been removed—who stood before God in perfection. Everything in me wanted to scream and curse and protest, but I was unable to utter a single sound. I just had to sit there and watch as God willingly forgave the sins of the high priest.

From this point forward, all my battles would be with the advocate— the Son of God. He is the perfect Joshua who takes away the sins of the world. In this courtroom moment I knew that in order to defeat God, I would have to defeat Jesus as the Son.

But I would need to be patient. God had already told Daniel the exact date that His advocate, the Messiah, the Christ, the Anointed One, would enter the world.

> *"Know and understand this: From the time the word goes out to restore and rebuild Jerusalem until the Anointed One, the ruler, comes, there will be seven 'sevens,' and sixty-two 'sevens.' It will be rebuilt with streets and a trench, but in times of trouble. After the sixty-two 'sevens,' the Anointed One will be put to death and will have nothing."*
>
> DANIEL 9:25–26

From the time of Cyrus's decree to restore and rebuild Jerusalem until the Anointed One arrived would be 483 years. I knew that, because God's spirit-being spokesman Gabriel said there would be seven plus sixty-two (69) "sevens." Simple math: 69 times 7 is always 483. Cyrus issued this decree, as is recorded in the first few verses of the writings of Ezra. Since God always keeps His promises, I knew I could observe and wait and see how the Anointed One would emerge.

In the interim, I would do everything in my power to ensure that as few people as possible—especially not the governors or the priests of Israel—would be ready on the day Christ came into the world. Was I successful? Oh yes. Read the records for yourself. A carpenter from Nazareth and his teenage bride-to-be knew. A few old people living in and around Jerusalem knew. Some astrologers from Persia knew. Know that I was watching very closely when the baby was born in Bethlehem—and I almost got Herod to kill Him. It would be another thirty years before I could arrange a wilderness meeting with "the final Joshua."

Joshua means "salvation." Did I mention that I hate that name?

Scripture references
[1]Genesis 6:9

6.
HEADLINE:
STANDOFF

The Bible states, "But when the set time had fully come, God sent his Son, born of a woman, born under the law" (Galatians 4:4) and that Son "being in very nature God, did not consider equality with God something to be used to his own advantage; rather, he made himself nothing by taking the very nature of a servant, being made in human likeness. And being found in appearance as a man, he humbled himself" (Philippians 2:6–8).

God selected the exact time in history

for the human birth of His Son, Jesus Christ. He selected the exact date, as He'd made clear through the prophet Daniel. The exact location in a specific city for the birth is known through the prophets Zechariah and Micah. God selected a specific man and woman—a carpenter from Nazareth named Joseph and his young bride-to-be, a virgin named Mary—to be the earthly parents of the Baby. Each year, near the end of the month of December, the Christian world expends much effort celebrating the event known as Advent or Christmas when "The Word became flesh and made his dwelling among us. We have seen his glory, the glory of the one and only Son, who came from the Father, full of grace and truth" (John 1:14).

With the exception of a few momentary glimpses, we are told little of the time between Jesus' birth and His baptism some thirty years later. God had provided a prophet, a relative of Jesus named John the Baptist, who preached for many days leading up to, and for a short time after, the beginning of Jesus' public ministry. At the age of thirty, Jesus began His public ministry by finding that prophet. John, who was preaching repentance and baptizing in the Jordan River near Jerusalem, introduced Jesus to his followers as the Son of God. Jesus asked John to baptize Him.

Then, according to the Gospel of Mark, "As Jesus was coming up out of the water, he saw heaven being torn open and the Spirit descending on him like a dove. And a voice came from heaven: 'You are my Son, whom I love; with you I am well pleased.' At once the Spirit sent him out into the wilderness, and he was in the wilderness forty days, being tempted by Satan. He was with the wild animals, and angels attended him" (Mark 1:10–13).

The Gospel of Matthew recounts the standoff in the wilderness between Jesus Christ, the Son of God, and the evil angel Satan, the adversary of God:

Then Jesus was led by the Spirit into the wilderness to be tempted by the devil. After fasting forty days and forty nights, he was hungry. The tempter came to him and said,

> *"If you are the Son of God, tell these stones to become bread."*
>
> *Jesus answered, "It is written: 'Man shall not live on bread alone, but on every word that comes from the mouth of God.'"*
>
> *Then the devil took him to the holy city and had him stand on the highest point of the temple. "If you are the Son of God," he said, "throw yourself down. For it is written: 'He will command his angels concerning you, and they will lift you up in their hands, so that you will not strike your foot against a stone.'"*
>
> *Jesus answered him, "It is also written: 'Do not put the Lord your God to the test.'"*
>
> *Again, the devil took him to a very high mountain and showed him all the kingdoms of the world and their splendor. "All this I will give you," he said, "if you will bow down and worship me."*
>
> *Jesus said to him, "Away from me, Satan! For it is written: 'Worship the Lord your God, and serve him only.'"*
>
> *Then the devil left him, and angels came and attended him.*
>
> MATTHEW 4:1–11

This reporter is aware that this standoff in the wilderness is perhaps the most significant confrontation in all history, a battle some four thousand years in the making. Not only did Satan desire this face-off, but God did, as well. I asked Satan to give us his recollections of this time in the wilderness, telling us what he'd hoped to accomplish as he came "face-to-face" with the Son of God, now in human form.

At the end of my first encounter with humanity—my triumph over Adam and Eve in the garden—God made a promise. Unfortunately for me, God always keeps His promises. He had told the man and the woman that one of their offspring would defeat me. From that point forward, I paid careful attention to the words God spoke, looking for clues as to just when that offspring would arrive and who that offspring would be.

I spent all of humanity's years waiting for this confrontation, preparing my plan to defeat God's "chosen one." Little by little, God gave clues to the humans who were recording His words. First, He told Abraham that this offspring would be one of his descendants.

Moses wrote that in the first book of the Law, in what you call Genesis, chapter 12. In that same book, chapter 49, it says the offspring would be from the tribe of Judah. Judah was one of Abraham's great grandchildren. Later, the prophet Samuel recorded the promise from God that King David, one of Judah's descendants, would be an ancestor of the promised offspring.[1]

Each time God identified ancestors, I did my best to mess them up. I might even have helped Abraham decide to sin in getting his wife's handmaiden pregnant! To this day, those who are sons of Abraham through his child Ishmael claim that one from their line will be the chosen offspring. Truly, anyone born through the line of Ishmael will be an imposter. But I've gotten millions to think otherwise.

I watched David commit adultery and I used this sin to try to distort the line God was forming. David paid greatly for that mistake, but God was still able to use him to continue the line through his son Solomon. Can you believe it?

Solomon was born to the wife of the man David murdered!

Eventually, the prophet Micah explained that the offspring would be born as a baby in Bethlehem, a small village to the south and west of Jerusalem, the hometown of David.[2] One of Isaiah's prophecies recorded that the baby would be born to a young woman who had never been intimate with a man—in other words, a "virgin birth."[3] The prophet Zechariah told of a man named Joshua—Yeshua in the original language—who would wear the crown of David. Right then, I understood that God's promised offspring would be given the name which means "the Lord is salvation." I remember telling you how much I hate that name.

The most helpful piece of information God gave about this offspring was through a Jewish prophet named Daniel. He was born in Jerusalem but was captured and eventually worked as an administrator in both the Babylonian and Medo-Persian Empires. Daniel prophesied that the offspring would be revealed exactly 483 years after a decree from Cyrus of Persia, allowing the Jewish people to return and resettle Jerusalem. Sure enough, the Son named "Yeshua" and born to a young virgin woman in Bethlehem arrived at the Jewish temple at the age of thirty-three, at the exact time God had promised through Daniel. I told you, though I hate to say it. . . God keeps His promises.

There is only one Person who fits God's promise. You know His name: Joshua when you translate from Hebrew. Jesus when you translate from Greek. God had sent His Son, completely human and yet, somehow, still fully God. They called His name Jesus, "because he will save his people from their sins."[4]

Jesus. Oh, how I hate that name!

I was ready when the young virgin gave birth. Men who knew Daniel's prophecy came from Persia to worship the Baby. I had placed a desire to kill the Baby in the heart of a ruler in Jerusalem— a man by the name of Herod. Herod was always spooked by conspiracies, and the report of the "one who has been born king of the Jews"[5] just put him over the edge. Once Herod's scholars confirmed the location and timing of the birth for themselves, Herod sent his soldiers to Bethlehem to kill the child. But he didn't know which one was the chosen one. So he instructed his men to kill every male child age two and under in that region! But the bumbler missed the offspring—Jesus' earthly family escaped with Him to Egypt.

I had been promised a confrontation, and it happened when the man born in Bethlehem began His public ministry. At the age of thirty, He appeared to a prophet named John, who baptized Jesus, while making a public announcement that Jesus was the offspring God had promised. John called Him "the Lamb of God, who takes away the sin of the world!"[6] I could barely stand the sound of those words.

But immediately after this, the Holy Spirit led Jesus into the wilderness area of Judea. This was to be our moment of confrontation!

Jesus found a spot to sit and wait

for me—and wait He did. I watched him from a distance for forty days. From time to time He would glance my way, but mostly He spent the time praying. Not once did He eat. He was definitely the Son of God, stronger than me—yet I knew the flesh He had encased Himself in would be weak after forty days without shelter and sustenance.

I knew Jesus would not turn from the work God had given Him. But I also knew about the other prophecies—like the one of Isaiah saying "he was led like a lamb to the slaughter"[7] and the one from Daniel about the Anointed One being "put to death."[8] I only hoped Jesus would realize that all this unpleasantness could be avoided—that the entire world and everyone in it could be His if only He would shift His allegiance from the heavenly Father to me.

So I started with His physical needs. He was obviously in pain from hunger, with His stomach somewhat bloated. He had lost at least twenty-five pounds from His strong carpenter frame. I reminded Him that the Son of God should not have to suffer such indignity. Why should one such as He be deprived? Why not tell the stones to become bread?

Naturally, He answered by quoting some obscure Bible verse. So I decided at that point to quote God's Word, as well. I took Jesus into Jerusalem and put Him on the most elevated point of the Temple Mount. There before us was all Jerusalem, the people below us worshipping God. I knew the rejection He was about to face. I knew they were going to mutilate His body. "Why not end it now?" I suggested. I told Jesus to throw Himself off the temple, allowing God to fulfill a promise of angels coming to Jesus' rescue. I hinted that such an impressive display would cause all Jerusalem to worship Him—but I would get the credit for initiating such a glorious moment.

But again, He refused me, speaking from that book God had written.

I thought carefully. He did not need food. He was not moved to action by the worshippers in Jerusalem. In that moment I knew I must offer Him everything.

Every knee on earth would bow to Him. Every tongue on earth would sing His name. I could arrange it all that very moment—if only He would bow His knee to me. He only had to do it once. He only had to do it for a moment. Only the heavenly Father and I would see it. If He only bowed to me once, I would be satisfied.

And then, for the third time, He spouted a line from scripture. Uggh! He would have to do it His own way.

Fine, let Him try to save the world His way. I offered Him the easy path. He chose the narrow way. Let Him go have His work on earth. I will find every way I can to oppose Him while He is in that body.

Scripture references

[1]2 Samuel 7:12–13
[2]Micah 5:2
[3]Isaiah 7:14
[4]Matthew 1:21
[5]Matthew 2:2
[6]John 1:29
[7]Isaiah 53:7
[8]Daniel 9:26

7.
HEADLINE:
INFLUENCE

Jesus' public ministry lasted approximately three years. During this time, He moved from town to town throughout Judea, preaching and teaching on mountainsides and in synagogues. He preached in grand locations, such as the Temple Mount in Jerusalem, and in humble surroundings, such as the home of a tax collector.

The Gospels tell us that Jesus was also well known for His miracles of healing. One time, Jesus spit in the dirt and made healing mud for a blind man. Another time, He told a crippled man to rise and walk. Ten lepers were healed and allowed to return to normal society. Several individuals had died or were very near death, and Jesus restored their lives and health completely.

Jesus also demonstrated His power by controlling nature. He walked on water. He commanded violent storms to cease. He took the lunch of a small boy and used it to feed thousands who had come to hear Him preach.

With all these things, Jesus developed a large group of followers. There were the thousands who followed Him, hoping to have their stomachs filled or their infirmities healed. In cities like Capernaum and Bethany, many people would host Jesus and His closest disciples when they were in their area. Those disciples—a collection of twelve men, handpicked by Jesus at the beginning of His three-year public ministry—traveled with Jesus till the end.

The Twelve are well-known, but two of them had very specific encounters with the adversary of God. Matthew 16 speaks of the leader of the disciples, Peter, while Luke 22 speaks of another respected disciple, Judas Iscariot, the one who was trusted with the finances of the ministry.

When Jesus came to the region of Caesarea Philippi, he asked his disciples, "Who do people say the Son of Man is?"

They replied, "Some say John the Baptist; others say Elijah; and still others, Jeremiah or one of the prophets."

"But what about you?" he asked. "Who do you say I am?"

Simon Peter answered, "You are the Messiah, the Son of the living God."

Jesus replied, "Blessed are you, Simon son of Jonah, for this was not revealed to you by flesh and blood, but by my Father in heaven. And I tell you that you are Peter, and on this rock I will build my church, and the gates of Hades will not overcome it. I will give you the keys of the kingdom of heaven; whatever you bind on earth will be bound in heaven, and whatever you loose on earth will be loosed in heaven." Then he ordered his disciples not to tell anyone that he was the Messiah.

From that time on Jesus began to explain to his disciples that he must go to Jerusalem and suffer many things at the hands of the elders, the chief priests and the teachers of the law, and that he must be killed and on the third day be raised to life.

Peter took him aside and began to rebuke him. "Never, Lord!" he said. "This shall never happen to you!"

Jesus turned and said to Peter, "Get behind me, Satan! You are a stumbling block to me; you do not have in mind the concerns of God, but merely human concerns."

Then Jesus said to his disciples, "Whoever wants to be my disciple must deny themselves and take up their cross and follow me. For whoever wants to save their life will lose it, but whoever loses their life for me will find it. What good will it be for someone to gain the whole world, yet forfeit their soul? Or what can anyone give in exchange for their soul? For the Son of Man is going to come in his Father's glory with his angels, and then he will reward each person according to what they have done. Truly I tell you, some who are standing here will not taste death before they see the Son of Man coming in his kingdom."

MATTHEW 16:13–28

Now the Festival of Unleavened Bread, called the Passover, was approaching, and

the chief priests and the teachers of the law
were looking for some way to get rid of Jesus,
for they were afraid of the people. Then Sa-
tan entered Judas, called Iscariot, one of the
Twelve. And Judas went to the chief priests
and the officers of the temple guard and dis-
cussed with them how he might betray Jesus.
They were delighted and agreed to give him
money. He consented, and watched for an
opportunity to hand Jesus over to them when
no crowd was present.

LUKE 22:1–6

This reporter took the opportunity to ask Satan about the three years of Jesus' public ministry, and in particular, about his specific interaction with two of Jesus' disciples, Simon Peter and Judas Iscariot.

Following our standoff in the wilderness, I watched with great interest as the Son of God spent three years moving through Galilee and Judea. I was surprised when He chose twelve somewhat pathetic human males to leave their jobs and their lives and travel with Him. They were certainly a strange

79

group. Several had been fisherman, which makes sense if you need food. One was a tax collector, hated in almost every area where the group travelled. Another was known as a Zealot, a political party that desired the overthrow of the Roman government. I knew from reading God's book that He intended for His Son to have an earthly throne and kingdom, but I did not see how it could happen if this motley collection of twelve were to be His inner circle.

I immediately began to study these twelve closely and found several who could be turned away from Jesus, if needed. The one named Simon (later known as Peter) stood out, because he seemed always to want to be the leader of the group. He was quick to pipe up and offer his opinion without much thought. Maybe Peter or his brother Andrew, also in the group, would stand and oppose Jesus if I needed them to. Another set of brothers, James and John, also wanted to be in charge of the group, so perhaps I could create conflict between them and Peter and Andrew. I knew I could influence these four brash and unrefined fishermen to be an embarrassment to Jesus.

Then I studied the others. It was easy to create conflict with the tax collector named Matthew and the Zealot, also named Simon. Matthew worked closely with the Roman government and Simon, as I mentioned, wanted to overthrow that government, viewing Jews like Matthew as traitors. One of the twelve was named Thomas, and he questioned everything—seemingly trusted no one. Perhaps he could cause conflict with his pessimism!

I saw great potential for turning the one named Judas Iscariot. He was quiet and backward, yet they had given him the chore of holding and managing their money. And there were four others, but they seemed content just to follow along and see what happened. I had no doubt that one or more of these twelve could be used to thwart the plans of God.

It was certainly easy to persuade the Jewish leaders, both political and religious, to oppose Jesus of Nazareth. All of them saw Him as a threat to their power and prestige. Unfortunately, a myriad of common people loved Jesus. They loved His preaching, teaching, and miracles. It seemed that whatever town He visited, the entire population would come out to greet Him. I was sickened each time Jesus went to a village where the leaders would not publicly oppose Him because of His popularity with the people. It soon became clear that I could not defeat the purposes of God with just those in authority—I was going to have to turn one of Jesus' closest friends. I needed a defector from among the twelve.

During those three years, I stayed close by. I knew everything Jesus and His followers were doing. I was looking for the right opportunity to strike. I was quite interested when Jesus' preaching changed from the establishment of the kingdom of God to subtle hints about His own destruction. Jesus began to prepare the twelve men for the day when He would no longer be on earth with them. That was when the perfect moment arrived.

Jesus was meeting with the Twelve when He made a startling announcement: He named Peter as the leader of the group for the time after Jesus was gone. Jesus gave Peter the "keys of the kingdom of heaven,"[1] more power than had ever been given to any human. More power than even I had been given before the rebellion. The Son of God proclaimed Himself to His disciples as the Messiah but then told them to keep that news to themselves. Jesus then told the Twelve that He was going to suffer and die but be resurrected three days later.

In that moment, everything I had heard and read from God made sense. I now knew God's plan, and I knew I had to defeat it. I needed to stop Jesus from dying and taking His life back. Instantly, I made my way toward

Peter, the newly christened leader, and forced him to confront Jesus. I just took him, as I had with the serpent in the garden. It was a wonderful moment—I was able to manipulate Peter so easily. It was his body and mouth, but it was my voice and words: "This shall never happen to you!"[2]

Jesus snapped and looked at Peter, but He spoke to me. I had hoped Jesus would strike him down right there, just as the serpent had been struck down in Eden. But He didn't.

It soon became horribly obvious that I would be unable to stop the Son of God from laying down His life. Jesus and the Twelve moved south to Jerusalem for the Passover celebration and an obvious confrontation with the political and religious leaders I had been influencing. As I continued to study the Twelve, I sensed their growing frustration. One especially, Judas Iscariot, seemed particularly troubled by events. His frustration, plus his obvious love of money, allowed me to

place within his mind the idea of sell-
ing out his Master for a price.

Judas went to the religious rulers,
received a paltry sum of money, and on
the night of the Passover betrayed
Jesus with a kiss. Oh, how I delighted
in seeing Jesus betrayed by one of
His own! I had succeeded in finding
my traitor. Jewish leaders and their
temple guards arrested Jesus, who was
eventually beaten, mocked, and put on
trial like a worthless criminal.

To my great pleasure, all of Jesus' disciples, except the fisherman
named John, ran from Him like scared
little children. Peter even stood by a
fire within the city, trying to convince everyone that he had never met
Jesus! I kept sending people to the
fire to confront Peter, and he just
kept denying the Son of God, until he
finally even cursed the name of Jesus.

This was all wonderful. Since Jesus was determined to die, I eventually decided to help make it happen. He
was crucified on a Roman cross, killed

by the people He had come to rule as
their Messiah. I enjoyed watching the
woman who God used to be His mother on
earth, kneeling on the ground, moaning
and crying as He suffered. I especially
relished the event as the cherubim and
seraphim and other angels, normally
making their racket while worshipping
at the throne of God, silently observed
their Creator dying while nailed to a
slab of wood. I declared victory as
eleven out of His twelve disciples fled
from Him, embarrassed for people to know
they were His followers. My schemes to
turn Judas and to scatter His followers
had worked to perfection.

Jesus had said that He would be
resurrected in three days. Now I had
to wait and see, satisfied that I had
done all I could do to thwart God's
plans on Earth.

Scripture references
[1]Matthew 16:19
[2]Matthew 16:22

8.
HEADLINE:
TRAPPED

The defining event of human history centers on three days in Jerusalem and the death, burial, and resurrection of the Son of God, Jesus Christ. Prior to this central event, the Bible gives only basic information on the activities and role of God's adversary, known primarily as either Satan or the devil. Once the resurrection of Jesus has occurred, along with the sending of the Holy Spirit into the world some fifty days after, the activities and philosophy of Satan are given in great detail in the New Testament.

Three New Testament books speak to the work of Satan and the spirit-beings who follow him against those who are unsaved, often referred to as "the world." The Holy Spirit is calling the unsaved to faith in Jesus Christ, while at the same time Satan is influencing them to remain unsaved. Satan's goal in this new era is to keep all men and women trapped in the darkness of sin and away from the light of Jesus Christ and His Word.

Both Jesus Himself and the apostle Paul described this work of Satan:

"Listen then to what the parable of the sower means: When anyone hears the message about the kingdom and does not understand it, the evil one comes and snatches away what was sown in their heart. This is the seed sown along the path. . . . "

Then he left the crowd and went into the house. His disciples came to him and said, "Explain to us the parable of the weeds in the field." He answered, "The one who sowed the good seed is the Son of Man. The field is the world, and the good seed stands for the people of the kingdom. The weeds are the

people of the evil one, and the enemy who sows them is the devil. The harvest is the end of the age, and the harvesters are angels."
MATTHEW 13:18–19, 36–39

The god of this age has blinded the minds of unbelievers, so that they cannot see the light of the gospel that displays the glory of Christ, who is the image of God.
2 CORINTHIANS 4:4

Flee the evil desires of youth and pursue righteousness, faith, love and peace, along with those who call on the Lord out of a pure heart. Don't have anything to do with foolish and stupid arguments, because you know they produce quarrels. And the Lord's servant must not be quarrelsome but must be kind to everyone, able to teach, not resentful. Opponents must be gently instructed, in the hope that God will grant them repentance leading them to a knowledge of the truth, and that they will come to their senses and escape from the trap of the devil, who has taken them captive to do his will.
2 TIMOTHY 2:22–26

This reporter asked the evil one to explain his thinking as he observed the death, burial, and resurrection of Jesus Christ, and the sending of the Holy Spirit to those who would believe in Jesus Christ as Savior. I also asked what methods Satan might use in his attempt to defeat the spread of Christianity throughout the world.

Every spirit-being, whether for or against God, watched Jesus give up His life on a Roman cross outside Jerusalem. For the demons and me, it was the most amazing experience—to watch as God the Son suffered in His human body.

Yet there was something else going on in that moment, for while there were three hours of darkness over the earth, that darkness encompassed our spiritual existence as well. Something happened between God the Father and God the Son, for when the darkness lifted, Jesus said, "It is finished," then gave up His life. I did not yet know what exactly had happened, but God suffered—and that always pleases me.

Every spirit-being watched as Jesus' body was placed in a new tomb by two of His human followers and as the Son of God took His life back and came out of His tomb on the third day, just as He had promised. God always keeps His promises—and I hate Him for it.

We all watched as Jesus again met with His followers. He offered every one of them forgiveness for their betrayal. This caused the angels and the cherubim to sing out in worship to God, while my demons and I simply simmered in our ever-expanding hatred for Him.

Whatever had happened between God the Father and God the Son must have been resolved, for every spirit-being saw Jesus as He ascended into heaven and sat down at the right hand of the Father—the preeminent position in all creation. In all of this my anger grew. After all, that throne should be mine.

We all watched as Jesus' followers, a pitiful band of 120 men and women, gathered together in a room in Jerusalem around the Jewish holiday of Pentecost, waiting for Jesus to fulfill another promise. I spent the time scheming to derail this promise and break God's string of perfect fulfillment.

But then He did it again. Every spirit-being watched as Jesus kept His promise and sent the Holy Spirit to dwell within the souls of those 120 followers. In that instant, they were all changed. They now had a guide for their lives and a comforter who would help them in times of trouble. They were given a Counselor who would show them the correct way to serve and to worship God. Of course, throughout the years we had seen a smattering of humans who were filled with the Holy Spirit, but never this many and in one place. This would make my work much more difficult, because a human who has been given the Holy Spirit is a new creation, far better equipped to resist my schemes and temptations.

Even the one named Simon Peter, who had so wonderfully fallen under my influence just fifty days earlier, now stood and proclaimed that Jesus was the Christ, the one who had come from God to provide salvation. If I had a heart, his sermon would've been like a stake driven through it. We all watched as thousands believed in Jesus the Son of God. This was our ultimate nightmare, that so many would so quickly believe the truth about Jesus and be indwelled by the Holy Spirit.

This nightmare continued as thousands more humans believed the next day, and again the next. More and more were added to the assembly, the gathering of believers. This was infuriating! I watched, knowing my methods would have to change. From this point forward, I would need to plan and scheme against those who had yet to hear the news (what these new "Christians" called the "good news") that Jesus had risen from the dead.

But my schemes quickly proved effective, because so many of these humans are weak and foolish. I began by confusing those to whom the message was being preached, to blind as many as possible—and I experienced much success. Many chose to doubt the message as I planted questions in their minds and hearts: *Did Jesus really rise from the dead, or was it an unsubstantiated claim from His followers? Is salvation really possible for me, or am I just too evil to receive forgiveness?* I wanted to keep in darkness every individual possible. To reach my ultimate goal, the defeat of God, I needed to keep every human from hearing—and believing—the truth about Jesus.

Unfortunately, I could not keep everyone from hearing. The followers of Christ, filled with the power of my nemesis, the Holy Spirit, began to move out from Jerusalem, into Judea and Samaria. One named Phillip began to teach the Samaritans about Jesus and many of them believed. People who had been in Jerusalem to conduct business with the Roman Empire also heard about Jesus and took the news with them back to their home countries. In Jerusalem it was hard to ignore the thousands of men and women who were worshipping the name of Jesus. I was alarmed at how quickly I was losing control of these humans—my people! Jesus and His Spirit were stealing them right out of my grasp!

I instructed the spirit-beings who follow me to pursue those who were preaching and teaching about Jesus. As Jesus' followers would speak to groups of five or ten, sometimes even one hundred or more, my spirit-beings were always present—and we would do anything to distract those who heard the preachers. We would influence those in the crowd, prompting them to yell out in anger, or just remind them that they were too busy with life and simply walk away. We would influence our own followers to stand nearby and preach a message of wealth or prosperity—anything to diminish the truth about Jesus.

This message of this "good news about

Jesus" was like a seed. Once it took root in good soil, it was inevitable that the human would choose to believe in Jesus as the Son of God. I had to kill that seed as soon as I could, to keep the person from believing. It did not help my cause that the disciples of Jesus, the original twelve (or should I say eleven, since the traitor Judas Iscariot turned to serve me—then killed himself) were performing many of the same miracles Jesus had performed. This only added to the power of the message about Jesus. I needed to discount these miracles as unimportant or unimpressive.

Once I trap humans, I work with great effort to never let them go. I get them focused on denying or arguing against the obvious truth that Jesus is God. I'll do anything to keep them from understanding. For once they understood the truth about Jesus—a truth I find disgusting—they would never choose to serve me. I cannot allow that to happen.

Humans must never understand the

truth that Jesus loves them. They must never understand the truth that Jesus wishes to forgive them. They must never understand the truth that the Holy Spirit can bring them joy. They must never understand that they were created by God in His image, to worship Him and be in His presence for eternity.

For I want them to be mine for eternity—apart from God, His Son, and His Spirit. I want every human I can influence to share my existence and my future.

9.
HEADLINE:
SCHEMES

Once an individual chooses to respond to the Gospel message in faith, that one is called "born again" and a child of God. At that point, the Holy Spirit indwells the believer, and the person is saved. When an individual becomes a Christian it is a defeat for Satan in his ongoing battle with God.

This does not mean that Satan ends his efforts against the individual. Satan's goals and methodology change, but not his efforts. There are at least six New Testament passages where Satan and his followers take action against the saved. These passages give a complete picture of the work and schemes of the devil against those who are part of the body of Christ.

> *Finally, be strong in the Lord and in his mighty power. Put on the full armor of God, so that you can take your stand against the devil's schemes. For our struggle is not against flesh and blood, but against the rulers, against the authorities, against the powers of this dark world and against the spiritual forces of evil in the heavenly realms.*
>
> EPHESIANS 6:10–12

> *Be alert and of sober mind. Your enemy the devil prowls around like a roaring lion looking for someone to devour.*
>
> 1 PETER 5:8

> *Another reason I wrote you was to see if you would stand the test and be obedient in everything. Anyone you forgive, I also forgive. And what I have forgiven—if there was anything to forgive—I have forgiven in the sight of Christ for your sake, in order that*

Satan might not outwit us. For we are not unaware of his schemes.

2 CORINTHIANS 2:9–11

But, brothers and sisters, when we were orphaned by being separated from you for a short time (in person, not in thought), out of our intense longing we made every effort to see you. For we wanted to come to you— certainly I, Paul, did, again and again— but Satan blocked our way.

1 THESSALONIANS 2:17–18

To keep me from becoming conceited, I was given a thorn in my flesh, a messenger of Satan, to torment me. Three times I pleaded with the Lord to take it away from me. But he said to me, "My grace is sufficient for you, for my power is made perfect in weakness." Therefore I will boast all the more gladly about my weaknesses, so that Christ's power may rest on me. That is why, for Christ's sake, I delight in weaknesses, in insults, in hardships, in persecutions, in difficulties. For when I am weak, then I am strong.

2 CORINTHIANS 12:7–10

Now for the matters you wrote about: "It is good for a man not to have sexual relations with a woman." But since sexual immorality is occurring, each man should have sexual relations with his own wife, and each woman with her own husband. The husband should fulfill his marital duty to his wife, and likewise the wife to her husband. The wife does not have authority over her own body but yields it to her husband. In the same way, the husband does not have authority over his own body but yields it to his wife. Do not deprive each other except perhaps by mutual consent and for a time, so that you may devote yourselves to prayer. Then come together again so that Satan will not tempt you because of your lack of self-control.

1 Corinthians 7:1–5

This reporter asked Satan if he agreed with these descriptions of him in the Bible—that he is lying in wait, making schemes of evil and hatred against believers in Jesus Christ. If so, I also asked if he could give some examples of the traps he is setting. Finally, in this interview, I wanted to know if his methodology had changed at all since his encounter with Adam and Eve, the first humans.

I am the Power of This Dark World! Now that is a phrase from the Bible I love to hear over and over again. I am the spiritual force of evil in the heavenly realms. I embrace my role. I love my role. And the less you understand about my methods, the better it is for me.

I love to sneak around and cause trouble for believers in Jesus Christ. By stealth and by deception, by audacious lies and whispered doubts, I try to cause believers in Jesus Christ to sin, to commit treason—blatant treason—against their Savior.

Although I still do pursue those pitiful, weak humans who have run to God for protection, my battle is really against the Holy Spirit. When I am able to cause a believer—one in whom the Spirit lives—to sin, it is a victory for me in my eternal battle with God.

Oh, I take such pleasure in seeing the Holy Spirit grieved. I savor those moments when His fire is quenched. I've destroyed families, churches, and entire cities as a result of one Christian believer choosing to follow my will rather than that of the Holy Spirit. I feast on those opportunities!

To grieve or quench God's Spirit, I must put Christians in circumstances where they will choose to sin against God. I send out my demon forces to find places where we can set traps against unsuspecting and unprepared followers of Jesus. It is so satisfying when we snare one.

Can I describe my favorite kind of Christian? It's the one just going through life, minding his own business, "serving" God in what I'd describe as a careless, usually halfhearted manner. I'm talking about the Christian who desires all of God's blessings, but isn't concerned with obeying His commands. When he's ignoring the fellowship of other believers, thinking everything in his life is okay, that is exactly the time when we attack.

One roar from this lion—I do love

being a "roaring lion"—and we send those Christians running right into our trap. Suddenly, they are caught in sin! So often it is a sin that embarrasses their family or their church. Mmm, mmm, good. Devouring believers, rendering them ineffective in testimony or ministry, is one of my great pleasures. The demons and I celebrate with every successful sin trap we have set. And my appetite is insatiable.

Even in times when I cannot tempt believers into some embarrassing public sin, I work hard to prevent them from being in fellowship with other Christians. I want believers to be cut off from those who would honor God and teach the scriptures as God intends. I lure many humans into churches and organizations teaching a false "gospel"— fakes that I have designed. Anything to keep people from sharing the truth, the good news about Jesus.

Sometimes God allows me to torment believers, much in the same way I was allowed to torment Job. I take great satisfaction in seeing followers of Christ in intense pain. My gratification increases greatly when I can then convince the suffering believers to blame God for their troubles. That is one of my greatest traps—charging God for misery when I am the source! I get to cause them pain and keep them weak, just like I did with Paul the apostle. Though that kind of backfired on me, since Paul found that his weakness just allowed God's strength to come through. . . .[1]

I'll grudgingly admit that this man—Saul of Tarsus who became Paul the Apostle—was one of my biggest disappointments. One day, I've got him all worked up, and he is on his way to Damascus, ready to put believers in jail and oversee a process that would have them murdered. Out of nowhere, Jesus appeared to him while on that very assignment, and one of my most effective humans was taken from me. Saul had been persecuting believers in Jesus, and then he became one of them. Saul was stolen away from me by Jesus. But I never let Saul forget his betrayal. One of my followers was with him at all times, never allowing him even a moment of rest. I was able to keep Saul (or Paul—so confusing) from places of ministry. He wanted to travel to the church in Thessalonica, but I prevented that—and hurt him in the process. He called the affliction a "thorn in [his] flesh, a messenger of Satan."[2] Ah, another Bible phrase I love. I love to torment.

I have another great trap, that of sexuality. Paul wrote much about sex and sexual sin—odd, since he never married. He worked as hard to keep believers from sexual sin as I do to trap them into it. In his letter to the Galatian churches, Paul wrote of the obvious sins. Many of them are sexual in nature: immorality, impurity and debauchery, drunkenness and orgies. In his first letter to the Corinthians, he again mentioned sexual immorality, as well as adulterers, male prostitutes, and homosexual offenders as being wicked. If God says these are wicked behaviors, then I want to convince as many as possible that they are not wicked. Of course they're okay! I am for anything God is against.

I want husbands to be dissatisfied with their wives and wives dissatisfied with their husbands. I want unmarried believers, both men and women, to be unsatisfied with their current circumstances. I want none of them to be content. I want them looking to one side and to the other, wondering if they are missing something. I want them to destroy their lives thinking sexual thoughts that are not pleasing to God. I want them thinking that in some way God has refused them the life that they deserve. Oh yes, this is one of the greatest weapons I have devised, taking God's perfect gift of sexual oneness in marriage and perverting it.

I still go after believers the same way I went after Eve in the garden. After all these years, it still works quite well. With three simple questions,

I can turn believers away from serving their Savior.

Did God really say that? I question God's Word.

Did God really mean that? I question God's judgment.

Did God really want that? I question God's love.

I cannot understand God's actions. He actually seems to want what is best for you. He sent His Son, Jesus Christ, to die on the cross to pay the price for your sin. He sends His Spirit to help you and comfort you as you live life as a believer in Jesus Christ. His pure love and joy are always on display, and in my exalted opinion, are just bizarre. This is simply not me.

I want to destroy you, because you are the image of the one I hate. I long to exploit you and to grieve God. Enough said.

Scripture references
[1]2 Corinthians 12:9
[2]2 Corinthians 12:7

10.

HEADLINE:
COUNTERFEIT

The Bible describes one of Satan's schemes that will happen in the future. Satan will make a final attempt to confuse and deceive as many men and women as he can by introducing an individual who will proclaim himself as the chosen one from God.

This individual is connected to Satan in Revelation 13 and is described there first as "a beast coming out of the sea" and then as a "beast, coming out of the earth" (verses 1 and 11). Daniel described these events in his writings and referred to an individual who will set up "an abomination that causes desolation" (9:27). Jesus quoted Daniel as He taught His disciples about matters in the future and described the days of this individual's rule as "dreadful" (Matthew 24:19). Paul also taught about this individual, referring to him as "the man of lawlessness" (2 Thessalonians 2:3) and saying the arrival of this "lawless one" would be "in accordance with how Satan works" (2 Thessalonians 2:8–9). John referred to this individual as "antichrist" (1 John 2:22), and compared him to people of John's own day who had presented themselves as antichrist—those who lie and deny that Jesus is the Christ.

"Know and understand this: From the time the word goes out to restore and rebuild Jerusalem until the Anointed One, the ruler, comes, there will be seven 'sevens,' and sixty-two 'sevens.' It will be rebuilt with streets and a trench, but in times of trouble. After the sixty-two 'sevens,' the Anointed One will be put to death and will have nothing. The people of the ruler who will come will destroy the city and the sanctuary. The end will

come like a flood: War will continue until the end, and desolations have been decreed. He will confirm a covenant with many for one 'seven.' In the middle of the 'seven' he will put an end to sacrifice and offering. And at the temple he will set up an abomination that causes desolation, until the end that is decreed is poured out on him."

DANIEL 9:25–27

"So when you see standing in the holy place 'the abomination that causes desolation,' spoken of through the prophet Daniel—let the reader understand—then let those who are in Judea flee to the mountains. Let no one on the housetop go down to take anything out of the house. Let no one in the field go back to get their cloak. How dreadful it will be in those days for pregnant women and nursing mothers! Pray that your flight will not take place in winter or on the Sabbath. For then there will be great distress, unequaled from the beginning of the world until now—and never to be equaled again. If those days had not been cut short, no one would survive, but for the sake of the elect those days will be shortened. At that time if anyone says to you, 'Look, here is the Messiah!' or, 'There he is!' do not believe it. For false messiahs and false

prophets will appear and perform great signs and to deceive, if possible, even the elect. See, I have told you ahead of time."

MATTHEW 24:15–25

Concerning the coming of our Lord Jesus Christ and our being gathered to him, we ask you, brothers and sisters, not to become easily unsettled or alarmed by the teaching allegedly from us—whether by a prophecy or by word of mouth or by letter—asserting that the day of the Lord has already come. Don't let anyone deceive you in any way, for that day will not come until the rebellion occurs and the man of lawlessness is revealed, the man doomed to destruction. He will oppose and will exalt himself over everything that is called God or is worshiped, so that he sets himself up in God's temple, proclaiming himself to be God.

Don't you remember that when I was with you I used to tell you these things? And now you know what is holding him back, so that he may be revealed at the proper time. For the secret power of lawlessness is already at work; but the one who now holds it back will continue to do so till he is taken out of the way. And then the lawless one will be revealed, whom the Lord Jesus will overthrow

*with the breath of his mouth and destroy
by the splendor of his coming. The coming of
the lawless one will be in accordance with
how Satan works. He will use all sorts of
displays of power through signs and won-
ders that serve the lie, and all the ways that
wickedness deceives those who are perishing.
They perish because they refused to love the
truth and so be saved. For this reason God
sends them a powerful delusion so that they
will believe the lie and so that all will be
condemned who have not believed the truth
but have delighted in wickedness.*

2 THESSALONIANS 2:1–12

*Dear children, this is the last hour; and as
you have heard that the antichrist is coming,
even now many antichrists have come. This
is how we know it is the last hour. They went
out from us, but they did not really belong to
us. For if they had belonged to us, they would
have remained with us; but their going
showed that none of them belonged to us.*

*But you have an anointing from the
Holy One, and all of you know the truth. I
do not write to you because you do not know
the truth, but because you do know it and
because no lie comes from the truth. Who is
the liar? It is whoever denies that Jesus is the*

*Christ. Such a person is the antichrist—
denying the Father and the Son. No one who
denies the Son has the Father; whoever ac-
knowledges the Son has the Father also.*
I JOHN 2:18–23

*And I saw a beast coming out of the sea. It
had ten horns and seven heads, with ten
crowns on its horns, and on each head a blas-
phemous name. The beast I saw resembled
a leopard, but had feet like those of a bear
and a mouth like that of a lion. The dragon
gave the beast his power and his throne and
great authority. One of the heads of the beast
seemed to have had a fatal wound, but the
fatal wound had been healed. The whole
world was filled with wonder and followed
the beast. People worshiped the dragon because he had given authority to the beast,
and they also worshiped the beast and asked,
"Who is like the beast? Who can wage war
against it?"*

*The beast was given a mouth to utter
proud words and blasphemies and to exercise
its authority for forty-two months. It opened
its mouth to blaspheme God, and to slander
his name and his dwelling place and those
who live in heaven. It was given power to
wage war against God's holy people and to*

conquer them. And it was given authority over every tribe, people, language and nation. All inhabitants of the earth will worship the beast—all whose names have not been written in the Lamb's book of life, the Lamb who was slain from the creation of the world.

Whoever has ears, let them hear.

"If anyone is to go into captivity, into captivity they will go. If anyone is to be killed with the sword, with the sword they will be killed.

This calls for patient endurance and faithfulness on the part of God's people.

Then I saw a second beast, coming out of the earth. It had two horns like a lamb, but it spoke like a dragon. It exercised all the authority of the first beast on his behalf, and made the earth and its inhabitants worship the first beast, whose fatal wound had been healed. And it performed great signs, even causing fire to come down from heaven to the earth in full view of the people. Because of the signs it was given power to perform on behalf of the first beast, it deceived the inhabitants of the earth. It ordered them to set up an image in honor of the beast who was wounded by the sword and yet lived. The second beast was given power to give breath

> to the image of the first beast, so that the im-
> age could speak and cause all who refused to
> worship the image to be killed. It also forced
> all people, great and small, rich and poor,
> free and slave, to receive a mark on their
> right hands or on their foreheads, so that
> they could not buy or sell unless they had the
> mark, which is the name of the beast or the
> number of its name. This calls for wisdom.
> Let the person who has insight calculate the
> number of the beast, for it is the number of a
> man. That number is 666.
>
> REVELATION 13:1–18

This reporter is aware that many Bible teachers have offered speculations about these future events and also that Satan does not have complete knowledge of the future—only God knows the specifics of the events which are to come. I asked the devil about his plans for the future.

My greatest deception is yet to come. I will seek to fool the entire population of the world at one time, causing the vast majority of humans everywhere to place their faith in—and

give their lives to—a false messiah.
It will be the ultimate moment of my
wicked existence, the greatest victory
I will have in my ongoing battle with
the Creator of the universe.

This will be my best work ever.
I've already convinced small groups
and even entire nations to reject
faith in Jesus Christ. Still, none of
these victories will compare to the
moment when every knee will bow to my
forgery. Think of it—God's own creation turning against Him and worshipping a total fraud!

I have been planning this deception
for millennia. When that prophet Daniel wrote about my schemes, they had
already been around for many years. He
exposed my entire plan to the world,
but since so few humans read the
Hebrew scriptures, very few of them will
be prepared when I finally succeed.

With every passing generation,
I have had a false messiah ready to
go. As John wrote in one of his letters, I have brought many counterfeits

forward—whether through the nation of Israel or in the church formed after Jesus' resurrection. So far none of them have been universally accepted. But that day is coming.

The most exciting part of my plan is that my fake will be worshipped in Jerusalem! The Jewish people will even build a new temple for my deception to sit in and receive worship. That will be a wonderful time for me, the fulfillment of all I have ever hoped to accomplish. When the humans bow before my abomination, they will really be bowing before me. I will receive that worship with great pride. It will be adoration that should have been mine all along.

My brilliant deception will put every person living on the planet into slavery. We'll stamp them with the day of man's creation, the day of sin, the number 666. There will be no rest. Any human that refuses my mark will be executed. Families will be divided, and the price for claiming the name of

Jesus Christ will be an excruciating death.

The wars spurred by my false messiah will truly be spectacular. Brother will rise against brother. Friend against friend. To defeat their enemies, nations will form alliances then turn on each other. The carnage will leave the world ravaged, and my false messiah will be there to fill the void in leadership. Those stupid humans will follow him even though he will be the one causing them discomfort and pain! I'm projecting that at least half of those living on the earth will die in these wars. Humans will kill for the thrill of killing. It will be primal—and I will orchestrate every minute of it.

On another front, all commerce will go through my beast. Every national capital, every state capital will be rendered impotent. Elected leaders, kings, queens, and dictators will all bow at the feet of my deception. They will gladly surrender their treasuries and taxes in worship of my chosen one. Each one will stand before the world, blaspheme the one true God, and worship my beast. They will have no choice, as their subjects and citizens will demand it. What a sight it will be.

If I were a nice guy, I'd suggest you be on the lookout. I am so ready to set this plan into motion. Maybe today will be the day that I take over every political and economic system in the world. I've been close before.

One day soon this dream of mine will become your reality.

11.
HEADLINE:
JUDGMENT

Much time and thought is invested in the events of the future. Children dream of growing into adults, imagining their future career, spouse, and activities as grown-ups. Adults look forward to retirement or time with grandchildren. Many Christians have overcome the difficulties of earthly life by thinking of the promise of eternal life in heaven in the presence of Jesus Christ.

Several New Testament passages refer to the future of God's adversary. Christ's own words on the subject are recorded in the Gospels of Matthew and John. James and Jude wrote of God and His authority to punish Satan and the spirit-beings who followed him. Revelation gives specific details about the timing and intensity of the judgment that awaits demonic and satanic beings.

What is fascinating is that Satan knows his future. He is keenly aware that judgment awaits him. Despite this knowledge, Satan continues to hate and oppose God, to exist each day as the evil one. He refuses to change.

Only those in authority may pronounce judgment. Only God has authority over Satan and his followers. God has pronounced judgment, and it is recorded in the scriptures.

"When the Son of Man comes in his glory, and all the angels with him, he will sit on his glorious throne. All the nations will be gathered before him, and he will separate the people one from another as a shepherd separates the sheep from the goats. He will put the sheep on his right and the goats on his left.

"Then the King will say to those on his right, 'Come, you who are blessed by my Father; take your inheritance, the kingdom prepared for you since the creation of the world. For I was hungry and you gave me something to eat, I was thirsty and you gave me something to drink, I was a stranger and you invited me in, I needed clothes and you clothed me, I was sick and you looked after me, I was in prison and you came to visit me.'

"Then the righteous will answer him, 'Lord, when did we see you hungry and feed you, or thirsty and give you something to drink? When did we see you a stranger and invite you in, or needing clothes and clothe you? When did we see you sick or in prison and go to visit you?'

"The King will reply, 'Truly I tell you, whatever you did for one of the least of these brothers and sisters of mine, you did for me.'

"Then he will say to those on his left, 'Depart from me, you who are cursed, into the eternal fire prepared for the devil and his angels. For I was hungry and you gave me nothing to eat, I was thirsty and you gave me nothing to drink, I was a stranger and you did not invite me in, I needed clothes and you did not clothe me, I was sick and in prison and you did not look after me.'

"They also will answer, 'Lord, when did we see you hungry or thirsty or a stranger or needing clothes or sick or in prison, and did not help you?'

"He will reply, 'Truly I tell you, whatever you did not do for one of the least of these, you did not do for me.'

"Then they will go away to eternal punishment, but the righteous to eternal life."

MATTHEW 25:31–46

Now there were some Greeks among those who went up to worship at the festival. They came to Philip, who was from Bethsaida in Galilee, with a request. "Sir," they said, "we would like to see Jesus." Philip went to tell Andrew; Andrew and Philip in turn told Jesus.

Jesus replied, "The hour has come for the Son of Man to be glorified. Very truly I tell you, unless a kernel of wheat falls to the ground and dies, it remains only a single seed. But if it dies, it produces many seeds. Anyone who loves their life will lose it, while anyone who hates his life in this world will keep it for eternal life. Whoever serves me must follow me; and where I am, my servant also will be. My Father will honor the one who serves me.

"Now my soul is troubled, and what

shall I say? 'Father, save me from this hour'?
No, it was for this very reason I came to this
hour. Father, glorify your name!"

Then a voice came from heaven, "I have
glorified it, and will glorify it again." The
crowd that was there and heard it said it
had thundered; others said an angel had spoken to him.

Jesus said, "This voice was for your
benefit, not mine. Now is the time for judgment on this world; now the prince of this
world will be driven out. And I, when I am
lifted up from the earth, will draw all people
to myself." He said this to show the kind of
death he was going to die.

JOHN 12:20–33

You believe that there is one God. Good!
Even the demons believe that—and shudder.
JAMES 2:19

They went to Capernaum, and when the Sabbath came, Jesus went into the synagogue and
began to teach. The people were amazed at his
teaching, because he taught them as one who
had authority, not as the teachers of the law.
Just then a man in their synagogue who was
possessed by an impure spirit cried out, "What
do you want with us, Jesus of Nazareth?

Have you come to destroy us? I know who you are—the Holy One of God!"

"Be quiet!" said Jesus sternly. "Come out of him!" The impure spirit shook the man violently and came out of him with a shriek.

The people were all so amazed that they asked each other, "What is this? A new teaching—and with authority! He even gives orders to impure spirits and they obey him." News about him spread quickly over the whole region of Galilee.

MARK 1:21–28

Jesus withdrew with his disciples to the lake, and a large crowd from Galilee followed. When they heard about all he was doing, many people came to him from Judea, Jerusalem, Idumea, and the regions across the Jordan and around Tyre and Sidon. Because of the crowd he told his disciples to have a small boat ready for him, to keep the people from crowding him. For he had healed many, so that those with diseases were pushing forward to touch him. Whenever the impure spirits saw him, they fell down before him and cried out, "You are the Son of God." But he gave them strict orders not to tell others about him.

MARK 3:7–12

*Though you already know all this, I want
to remind you that the Lord at one time
delivered his people out of Egypt, but later
destroyed those who did not believe. And
the angels who did not keep their positions
of authority but abandoned their proper
dwelling—these he has kept in darkness,
bound with everlasting chains for judgment
on the great Day. In a similar way, Sodom
and Gomorrah and the surrounding towns
gave themselves up to sexual immorality and
perversion. They serve as an example of those
who suffer the punishment of eternal fire.*

JUDE 5–7

*And I saw an angel coming down out of
heaven, having the key to the Abyss and
holding in his hand a great chain. He seized
the dragon, that ancient serpent, who is the
devil, or Satan, and bound him for a thousand years. He threw him into the Abyss,
and locked and sealed it over him, to keep
him from deceiving the nations anymore until the thousand years were ended. After that,
he must be set free for a short time.*

*I saw thrones on which were seated
those who had been given authority to judge.
And I saw the souls of those who had been
beheaded because of their testimony about*

Jesus and because of the word of God. They had not worshiped the beast or its image and had not received its mark on their foreheads or their hands. They came to life and reigned with Christ a thousand years. (The rest of the dead did not come to life until the thousand years were ended.) This is the first resurrection. Blessed and holy are those who share in the first resurrection. The second death has no power over them, but they will be priests of God and of Christ and will reign with him for a thousand years.

When the thousand years are over, Satan will be released from his prison and will go out to deceive the nations in the four corners of the earth—Gog and Magog—and to gather them for battle. In number they are like the sand on the seashore. They marched across the breadth of the earth and surrounded the camp of God's people, the city he loves. But fire came down from heaven and devoured them. And the devil, who deceived them, was thrown into the lake of burning sulfur, where the beast and the false prophet had been thrown. They will be tormented day and night for ever and ever.

REVELATION 20:1–10

This reporter confronted Satan with this information about his ultimate end. His pride and defiance continued even when discussing this subject.

As much as I hate to admit it, I've always known my fate. The moment my heart filled with pride and I set my mind to defeat God, I knew what my final destiny would be. I watched God speak the lake of fire into existence. He did it the very moment I chose to rebel.

My followers also knew that God would punish us for eternity, that He would eventually cut us off and restrict us. Our ultimate demise was tasted during gut-wrenching moments of having to bow before the Son of God and worship Him, even in those years He lived in Palestine and walked the earth.

But I still had fight in me. That's why it became our goal and our mission to force God to punish with us as many of the humans He had created. Even though this coming punishment makes us shudder in fear, we put the future out of our minds and focus on the present mission. I have vowed to see things through to the end. I am determined to let nothing stop me.

Every day I cause people to deny their Creator.

Every day I cause people to deny their Savior.

Every day I cause people to deny their Comforter.

Oh, I have had a marvelous career. After my counterfeit is revealed, my work will be interrupted. However, God's Word says I get one more shot at His creation. And I will take full advantage of the opportunity.

If you think my plans and schemes have been ruthless up to this point, just wait. Yes, I will be thrown into an abyss for one thousand years. But then I will be released for a short time. With one thousand years to plan and scheme, I will be more than ready. I will cause such mayhem that the so-called perfect world Jesus is ruling will be thrown into chaos and tumult in only minutes.

I will once again split families. I will once again pit brother against brother and husband against wife and parents against children. I will once again bring neighbor against neighbor. It is who I am and it is what I do—and I will do it until the very last moment I am cast into my eternal flame. And I will have earned every moment of torment that I receive.

If I have to go down, I'll gladly take with me as many humans as possible—to experience for eternity the torment designed for me.

12.
HEADLINE:
RESISTANCE

Satan is not all-powerful. His schemes and efforts can be defeated. Four New Testament writers penned letters to their fellow believers with easy-to-follow instructions for defeating God's adversary. They are dealt with in this chapter in chronological order.

James wrote first about the defeat of Satan in chapter 4 of his letter to the persecuted Christian Jews who were scattered from Jerusalem. This letter was written at least fifteen years after the resurrection of Jesus Christ.

Paul wrote nearly ten to twelve years later while under house arrest in Rome. His letter to the church in Ephesus contains a six part solution to be used against the efforts of Satan.

Peter's New Testament letters were likely penned a few years after Paul's letter to the Ephesians and just a year or two before Peter's death. His readers are being persecuted by the government and are being tempted by Satan to live against God's principles. Peter gives simple instruction for Christians to use in the fight against the evil one.

John's letters, written nearly forty years after James's epistle, are the last books of the New Testament and mark the completion of scripture. He encourages believers in their daily effort to resist the devil.

Resistance is an important part of living as a Christian. Too often, well-intentioned people choose not to resist because they believe Satan to be too strong and powerful. We must remember that he is *not* God's equal. Satan is a created being who has already been easily defeated by

God on three occasions. First, Satan was defeated in the war of the spirit-beings, where he was cast out of heaven. Second, Satan was defeated by Jesus in the wilderness. Third, Satan was defeated when Jesus Christ was crucified, His death being found acceptable payment for the sin debt owed by all men and women. Thus sin, for which Satan is king, can be of no effect on those who have trusted Christ as Savior.

It should also be noted that the individual Christian does not resist Satan through enlightened human thought or personal strength and power. God has provided the blueprint for defeating Satan. God has sent His Holy Spirit, and the Spirit is the one who brings strength and power to the fight. God has also given us the Body of the Christ, other believers in Jesus Christ, who can encourage the individual Christian in this area of resistance.

What causes fights and quarrels among you? Don't they come from your desires that battle within you? You desire but do not have, so you kill. You covet but you cannot get what you want, so you quarrel and fight. You do not have because you do not ask God. When you ask, you do not receive, because you ask with wrong motives, that you may spend what you get on your pleasures.

You adulterous people, don't you know that friendship with the world means enmity against God? Therefore, anyone who chooses to be a friend of the world becomes an enemy of God. Or do you think Scripture says without reason that he jealously longs for the spirit he has caused to dwell in us envies intensely? But he gives us more grace. That is why Scripture says: "God opposes the proud but shows favor to the humble."

Submit yourselves, then, to God. Resist the devil, and he will flee from you. Come near to God and he will come near to you. Wash your hands, you sinners, and purify your hearts, you double-minded. Grieve, mourn and wail. Change your laughter to mourning and your joy to gloom. Humble yourselves before the Lord, and he will lift you up.

JAMES 4:1–10

Finally, be strong in the Lord and in his mighty power. Put on the full armor of God, so that you can take your stand against the devil's schemes. For our struggle is not against flesh and blood, but against the rulers, against the authorities, against the powers of this dark world and against the spiritual forces of evil in the heavenly realms. Therefore put on the full armor of God, so that when the day of evil comes, you may be able to stand your ground, and after you have done everything, to stand. Stand firm then, with the belt of truth buckled around your waist, with the breastplate of righteousness in place, and with your feet fitted with the readiness that comes from the gospel of peace. In addition to all this, take up the shield of faith, with which you can extinguish all the flaming arrows of the evil one. Take the helmet of salvation and the sword of the Spirit, which is the word of God. And pray in the Spirit on all occasions with all kinds of prayers and requests. With this in mind, be alert and always keep on praying for all the Lord's people.

Pray also for me, that whenever I speak, words may be given me so that I will fearlessly make known the mystery of the gospel, for which I am an ambassador in chains. Pray that I may declare it fearlessly, as I should.

EPHESIANS 6:10–20

To the elders among you, I appeal as a fellow elder and a witness of Christ's sufferings who also will share in the glory to be revealed: Be shepherds of God's flock that is under your care, watching over them—not because you must, but because you are willing, as God wants you to be; not pursuing dishonest gain, but eager to serve; not lording it over those entrusted to you, but being examples to the flock. And when the Chief Shepherd appears, you will receive the crown of glory that will never fade away.

In the same way, you who are younger, submit yourselves to your elders. All of you, clothe yourselves with humility toward one another, because, "God opposes the proud but shows favor to the humble."

Humble yourselves, therefore, under God's mighty hand, that he may lift you up in due time. Cast all your anxiety on him because he cares for you.

Be alert and of sober mind. Your enemy the devil prowls around like a roaring lion looking for someone to devour. Resist him, standing firm in the faith, because you know that the family of believers throughout the world is undergoing the same kind of sufferings.

And the God of all grace, who called you

*to his eternal glory in Christ, after you have
suffered a little while, will himself restore you
and make you strong, firm and steadfast. To
him be the power for ever and ever. Amen.*

1 PETER 5:1–11

*Everyone who sins breaks the law; in fact,
sin is lawlessness. But you know that [Jesus Christ] appeared so that he might take
away our sins. And in him is no sin. No one
who lives in him keeps on sinning. No one
who continues to sin has either seen him or
known him.*

*Dear children, do not let anyone lead
you astray. The one who does what is right is
righteous, just as he is righteous. The one who
does what is sinful is of the devil, because
the devil has been sinning from the beginning. The reason the Son of God appeared
was to destroy the devil's work. No one who
is born of God will continue to sin, because
God's seed remains in him; they cannot go
on sinning, because they have been born of
God. This is how we know who the children
of God are and who the children of the devil
are: Anyone who does not do what is right is
not God's child, nor is anyone who does not
love their brother and sister.*

1 JOHN 3:4–10

This reporter asked Satan about the tactics he uses in his battle against humanity. I wanted to know what "big ideas" he had in mind.

You probably think I spend all my time plotting major cataclysmic events on a worldwide scale, and there is some truth in that. But I actually spend most of my time scheming to keep people from reading and understanding God's Word. My goal is simple—and I am glad you humans continue to fall for it so often. I want you to reject God by denying Jesus Christ is the Son of God—and by resisting the work of the Holy Spirit in your life. I hate that I cannot gain victory over God. . . but I can gain victory over you.

Here is what is perhaps my favorite lie for you silly humans: You do not need the Bible or Jesus Christ or the Holy Spirit to live a life pleasing to God. Ah, it's wonderful that so many of you accept this fallacy as fact!

That New Testament letter from James contains a piece of truth that I hope you never understand. When left to your own thoughts and desires, your motives will always be like mine—greedy, selfish, troublemaking—all things that I love. Your motives will not please God unless you submit yourself to God by moving closer to Him. You do that by reading the Bible, trusting Jesus Christ, and following the leading of the Holy Spirit. Of course, I want you to avoid the Bible, to distrust Jesus Christ, and to ignore the Holy Spirit. Just look around the world. I am pretty good at motivating humans to steer clear of Christ!

I need you to always be in conflict, at war, in fights and quarrels. I need you to be in conflict with those who are in authority over you, whether it is a parent, a teacher, a boss, a spouse, government officials, or a spiritual leader. I need you always off-balance, always in a state of want. When you are in that condition, it makes me sneer with glee.

I want you to look at those around you and be jealous—a have-not. When this happens, I want you to blame God and be in conflict with Him. I know it is illogical—but you humans love to play the blame game. It's almost irresistible.

James wrote that God gives grace to the humble and resists the proud. I need to keep appealing to you and your pride. I need you to constantly be focused on what you want, what you think you need, making demands of God, rather than asking for His will to be done. I need you to go to God in anger and envy, insisting He do what you wish. When you do that, I have you right where I want you. Because then you are submitting to me, rather than to God.

James asks you to be upset about your sin, to confess it, to find ways to eliminate it from your life. I want you to see your sin as normal—as your right—and I want you to revel in it. I want you to wallow in pride and conflict. I want you to resist God.

It is crushing to me when an individual chooses to be humble before God or to seek out wisdom found in His Word. I have to cover my ears when an individual speaks to God and says, "I am a sinner and I need your forgiveness." I need you in gloom and mourning—but if your sins are forgiven you will experience joy and laughter. When you're in that state, I cannot control you.

I don't want you listening to James and I certainly don't want you following the advice Paul gives in his letter to the Ephesians. If you listen to Paul, you will understand that I am at war with God by being at war with you.

I present myself to you as a harmless guest. Think of me as a friend you cannot live without. Trust me. If you forget that I am at war with God, you'll likely forget that I actually wish to destroy you, your life, and your family. Maybe I've spoken too much truth here. Really. . .I want you to forget the truth about me and ignore the truth about God.

Paul wants you to dress for battle. Using the standard uniform of the Roman soldier, he provides the believer in Jesus Christ with a picture of how to defend against my attacks, which he calls "flaming arrows."[1] His list of armor reflects the character of God, and since I despise God, I despise these concepts, as well.

I don't want you considering the truth from God and His Word. I want you following my lies. I don't want you thinking about righteousness; I want you seeking ways to sin. I don't want you living in peace, but in conflict with God and with the humans around you. I don't mind if you "have faith"—but I want your faith to be in me or some other object, anything other than in God or His Son. I certainly don't want you thinking about salvation. I want you trapped and enslaved in your doubts and your fears.

Let's not even talk about the sword of the Spirit, which is the Word of God. I don't want you anywhere near that book. No praying either, not to God or in the name of Jesus or the power of God's Spirit. I just do not want you dressed for battle. I want my arrows to hit the bull's-eye every time. I want you to be miserable and unable to defend yourself. I want you to ignore the armor God has provided for you. I want you weak and afraid.

Not only does God want you coming near to Him and want you wearing His armor, but He wants you to understand that He has provided other Christians to help you resist my schemes and my arrows. Peter wrote about this in his letters to the church.

God has provided every Christian with other Christians who are given the responsibility of leadership in the church. Whether you call them overseers, elders, or pastors, these individuals serve God's purpose of teaching the Word of God to other

believers and guiding a group of believers through life. For me to hurt
God, I must destroy these overseers,
and I must work to put you in conflict
with them as well. I take great joy in
this type of destruction. I love it
when one group of Christians is fight-
ing with another. After all, chaos is
my specialty. I stir things up everywhere I can.

Peter's description of me in his
letter is easily my favorite: "A roaring
lion looking for someone to devour."[2]
I love that line. It is perfectly me,
a description of all that I am. I am
always looking for someone to devour.
Have you ever seen a lion just rip
the flesh away from an animal that
has been captured? That is my desire
for you, my precious prey. I want to
rip you apart, piece by piece, until
there is nothing left of you but rot-
ting bones.

Peter's remedy for my lying in wait
is to stand firm in the faith, to be
self-controlled and alert. As long as

I have you disrespecting your God-given overseers, living in conflict within your church, you cannot possibly be self-controlled and alert. In that moment, I have you. I just have to wait for the right moment, the moment you are least expecting it, and I will pounce. And you will be. . . ripped apart by me.

John was the last of the New Testament writers. He was speaking of me when he said, "Do not let anyone lead you astray."[3] Confusing the understanding of God's Word and sending humans in the wrong direction has always been my thing. One of my greatest accomplishments is when a human commits sin and then stands up and calls it righteousness. Believe me when I tell you that Christians are sinning every moment of every day, then praising God for their ability to do so. Those are things I love to hear!

The most significant part of resistance to me is right there in the words John wrote. "The reason the Son of God appeared was to destroy the devil's work."[4] And the truth is Jesus Christ did destroy my work. A human does not have to be under my influence at all. The human can know Jesus Christ as Savior, be filled with the Holy Spirit, and draw near to God. The human who humbly submits himself to God in this way will have little problem with me—I actually have to run away from that one.

Please do me a favor: Don't tell anyone. It would cause me big problems if word of this ever got out. Why, if humans started resisting me and following God, the world as we know it would be ruined. I would be ruined. Jesus would be praised, and I'd hate that because I hate Him.

And because of Him. . .I hate you.

Scripture references

[1] Ephesians 6:16

[2] 1 Peter 5:8

[3] 1 John 3:7

[4] 1 John 3:8

13

HEADLINE:

CHOICES

This reporter trusts that you are now fully aware of the truth about Satan.

Satan is quite literally God's adversary, a sworn enemy who will not cease combat against God until the day he is cast into the lake of fire.

Because you were made in the image of God, Satan hates you, whether you are a believer in Jesus Christ or not. The evil one wishes to destroy your life, first and foremost, by keeping you from worshipping God.

Satan desires that you spend eternity with him in the lake of fire, where you will be separated from God forever and ever.

In his letter to the Philippians the apostle Paul made this appeal:

Not that I have already obtained all this, or have already arrived at my goal, but I press on to take hold of that for which Christ Jesus took hold of me. Brothers and sisters, I do not consider myself yet to have taken hold of it. But one thing I do: Forgetting what is behind and straining toward what is ahead, I press on toward the goal to win the prize for which God has called me heavenward in Christ Jesus.

All of us, then, who are mature should take such a view of things. And if on some point you think differently, that too God will make clear to you. Only let us live up to what we have already attained.

Join together in following my example, brothers and sisters, and just as you have us as a model, keep your eyes on those who live as we do. For, as I have often told you before and now tell you again even with tears, many live as enemies of the cross of Christ. Their destiny is destruction, their god is their stomach, and their glory is in their shame. Their mind is set on earthly things. But our citizenship is in heaven. And we eagerly await a Savior from there, the Lord Jesus Christ, who, by the power that enables him to bring everything under his control, will transform our lowly bodies so that they will be like his glorious body.

Therefore, my brothers and sisters, you whom I love and long for, my joy and crown, stand firm in the Lord in this way, dear friends!

PHILIPPIANS 3:12–4:1

This reporter would direct your attention to verse 18 in this passage: "many live as enemies of the cross of Christ." Certainly, Satan is one of the "many."

Satan is an enemy. His destiny is destruction. His god is his stomach—in other words, his own satisfaction. Even though Satan is filled with pride in his own being, he truly lives a life of shame.

Satan has already described for you the choice that Paul made in his life. In these verses from Philippians, Paul notes that "Christ Jesus took hold of me" (Philippians 3:12). Jesus confronted Paul with the fact that Paul was a sinner who needed a Savior, and Paul believed. He ceased serving the evil one and began serving Jesus.

If you are reading this book and are unsure about the identity of Jesus Christ, this reporter prays that you will read the next few verses and choose to believe what Jesus said about Himself.

"For God so loved the world that he gave his one and only Son, that whoever believes in him shall not perish but have eternal life. For God did not send his Son into the world to condemn the world, but to save the world through him. Whoever believes in him is not condemned, but whoever does not believe stands condemned already because they have not believed in the name of God's one and only Son. This is the verdict: Light has come into the world, but people loved darkness instead of light because their deeds were evil. Everyone who does evil hates the light, and will not come into the light for fear that their deeds will be exposed. But whoever lives by the truth comes into the light, so that it may be seen plainly that what they have done has been done in the sight of God."

JOHN 3:16–21

Jesus Christ, the one and only Son of God, came into the world as the Light of the World. Every human must choose to follow one of two paths: the path of evil and darkness as laid out by Satan; or the path of truth and light as laid out by Jesus Christ. One leads to an abyss, the other to heaven on earth. Salvation is offered to every human by God through faith in Jesus Christ.

This reporter is also praying for my Christian friends who have read this interview. I remind you that Satan is not God's equal. He is a created being who can be defeated easily if a believer will submit to God's Word and follow the plans for resistance as found in the New Testament.

Christian friend, you are a citizen of heaven, just as Paul describes in Philippians 3:20. All believers should be eagerly living for the glory of the Savior Jesus Christ and standing firm in Him. Although Satan is going to throw scheme after scheme in your direction, you can live your life like Paul, "forgetting what is behind"—a sinful, Satan-serving past—and "straining toward what is ahead" (Philippians 3:13).

Always remember James 4:7—"Submit yourselves, then, to God. Resist the devil, and he will flee from you."

About the Author

Russell Wight has served Jesus Christ as a Bible teacher since 1987 in over 300 churches through camps, kids clubs, and pulpits. He lives with his wife and three children on Cape Cod, Massachusetts.

Contact the Author

E-mail: interviewwiththedevil@gmail.com
Twitter: @RussellWight1

ALSO FROM
BARBOUR PUBLISHING

Here's a million-copy
bestseller made even
better: *Know Your Bible*
is a concise, easy-to-
understand guide to
God's Word—and
now it's illustrated
in full color! Giving
you a helpful and
memorable overview
of each of scripture's
66 books, *Know Your
Bible* provides data on
the author and time frame, a ten-word synopsis,
a longer (50–100 word) summary, thoughts
on what makes the book unique or unusual, a
listing of key verses, and a "So, What?" section
of practical application. Packed with informative
and intriguing photos and paintings, it's a
fantastic resource for individuals and ministries!

ISBN 978-1-61626-710-0
4.25" x 7" / 144 pages

Available wherever Christian books are sold.